The UK's Relationship with Europe

John Todd

The UK's Relationship with Europe

Struggling over Sovereignty

John Todd
Department of Criminology and Sociology of
Law and ARENA Centre for European Studies
University of Oslo
Oslo, Norway

ISBN 978-3-319-33668-8   ISBN 978-3-319-33669-5   (eBook)
DOI 10.1007/978-3-319-33669-5

Library of Congress Control Number: 2016944507

Printed on acid-free paper

This Palgrave Macmillan imprint is published by Springer Nature
The registered company is Springer International Publishing AG Switzerland

ACKNOWLEDGMENTS

This book has been written with the support of a number of academic institutions. These institutions all share an open and supportive environment, with a focus on producing high-quality research. They are, in roughly chronological order, the Norwegian University of Life Sciences (NMBU), The Norwegian Institute of International Affairs (NUPI), the ARENA Centre of European Studies, and the Department of Criminology and Sociology of Law at the University of Oslo. I am particularly grateful for the sage advice and feedback from Nina Græger at NUPI and Chris Lord at ARENA. Stig Jarle Hansen, Benjamin de Carvalho, and Halvard Leira also deserve thanks for helping my transition from the world of policy to the world of research. This work benefitted greatly from the comments of Paul Beaumont at NMBU, Kristin Haugevik at NUPI, and the anonymous reviewers.

Finally, a huge thank you to Mari—I couldn't have done it without you!

An earlier version of this book was published as a research report by the ARENA Centre for European Studies, University of Oslo.

CONTENTS

LIST OF FIGURES

LIST OF TABLE

CHAPTER 1

Introduction

Abstract The UK's volatile relationship with Europe matters. It matters for the UK, it matters for the European Union (EU), and it matters for the fortunes of the UK's political leaders. This book is inspired by the potential for dramatic change in the UK–EU relationship following David Cameron's commitment to hold an in/out referendum on EU membership. The introductory chapter sets out the rationale and context for the book in these terms, noting the relevance of exploring how political and the media discourse on Europe has evolved over the past 40 years.

Keywords Euroscepticism • Referendum • Discourse analysis • Sovereignty

The UK's relationship with Europe matters. It matters for the UK, it matters for the European Union (EU), and it matters for the fortunes of the UK's political leaders. Indeed, two of the UK's most famous Prime Ministers were hugely affected by challenges emanating from continental Europe; such challenges were the making of Churchill and the breaking of Thatcher. The relationship between the UK and the EU has the potential for dramatic change following David Cameron's commitment to hold an in/out referendum on EU membership. This book studies the evolution of the British discourse on Europe since the 1970s. Analysing the British discourse on Europe, including the increasing prominence of immigration issues, will help us understand how the referendum commitment became

J. Todd, *The UK's Relationship with Europe*,
DOI 10.1007/978-3-319-33669-5_1

1

possible and propose some implications for the referendum campaign itself. In theoretical terms, I hope to demonstrate that poststructuralist discourse analysis can provide interesting, accessible, and useful insights into questions of foreign policy and identity.

1.1   CONTEXT AND JUSTIFICATION: WHY NOW?

Europe has always been of critical importance for the future of the UK, with a history of migration, invasion, and power-balancing, which has caused much strife for people and politicians alike. Throughout history, Europe has been the UK's biggest trading partner and an occasional source of existential threat (be this threat Napoleonic France or Nazi Germany). European issues of one sort or another have, therefore, never been too far from the top of the British political agenda. The relationship issues have continued to trouble the political leaders of the UK even after the country joined the European Economic Community (EEC) in 1973. The UK has come to be regarded as an "awkward partner" in the project of European integration (Daddow 2006:311; George 1998) and the "home of the term Euroscepticism" (Spiering 2004:127). Nigel Farage and his populist United Kingdom Independence Party (UKIP) are employing the issue of Europe to mount, what has been termed by Professor John Curtice, "the most serious fourth party incursion" into English politics since the Second World War (quoted in Watt 2013).In an example of history rhyming, if not quite repeating, David Cameron echoed his Labour predecessor Harold Wilson by announcing, in January 2013, his intention to hold an in/out referendum on EU membership in 2017 following negotiation of "a new settlement with our European partners" (Cameron 2013). Obviously, a referendum could result in a vote in favour of leaving the EU—a "Brexit"—and thus to massive and fundamental change for both the UK and the EU itself. The struggle between those striving to escape the dark and cloying embrace of Brussels to the post-Brexit sunlit uplands and those concerned about the UK drifting off into a less than splendid mid-Atlantic isolation will only become more intense as the referendum approaches.

David Cameron's premiership has already witnessed an increasingly frenetic debate on the UK's membership of the EU. During the early period of his term of office, Eurosceptic Conservative Members of Parliament applied sustained pressure on the Prime Minister with the aim of securing a referendum on EU membership. These MPs had been disappointed and angered that the Prime Minister had decided against holding a referendum on the Treaty of Lisbon.[1] They were also worried about UKIP's strong performance in the opinion polls under the flamboyant Mr Farage. Nearly 100 of these Conservative MPs signed their names to a letter to the Prime Minister in summer 2012 that urged him to hold a referendum (see Montgomerie 2012). The pressure was kept up through the rest of the year, with the Prime Minister eventually making his referendum speech in January 2013. This speech made two important commitments. First, to renegotiate the relationship between the UK and the EU, and second, should the Conservatives win the next general election, to hold an in/out referendum on the UK's continued membership of the EU (Cameron 2013). Unfortunately for the Prime Minister, these commitments incited, rather than appeased, his backbenchers, and UKIP continued to perform well in the polls. With regard to the former point, a ComRes poll at the end of May 2013 found that approximately 56 % of voters believed the Conservatives were at that point more divided than they were during the internecine struggles of the Maastricht debates in the early 1990s (reported in Mason 2013).

Regarding immigration, Carey and Geddes (2010:851) observe that there is a strong connection between immigration and European integration because the UK has been the destination for much intra-EU migration. An illustration of the current salience of the immigration issue in connection with the EU is a November 2015 YouGov poll, in which respondents were asked: "When renegotiating Britain's relationship with the EU, in which if any of the following areas do you think David Cameron should seek to change our relationship with the EU?" The top issue for respondents was "Greater control of our borders and immigration from the EU," with "Limits on welfare benefits EU migrants to Britain are eligible for" coming in second (YouGov 2015:5; see also YouGov 2014:7).

It is therefore timely to study the European discourse in the UK. Whilst, historically, European issues are rarely on top of the list of voters' concerns, related issues like immigration and the economy are. Also, the issue of Europe is associated with a highly contested discourse, where the success or failure of politicians' arguments has potentially major implications, both for the future of the UK's relationship with the EU and for the prospects of the politicians themselves. With the referendum approaching, there is certainly significant scope to analyse how key actors seek to make arguments and shape narratives to influence British policy towards the EU.

1.2   Aims/Objectives

This book aims to analyse the drawing of social boundaries in the British discourse about Europe. In particular, I intend to analyse how the discourse has evolved since the UK joined the EEC in 1973, including emphasising the role of immigration within the discourse on Europe. On the basis of the discourse analysis, I aim to draw out some implications for how the relationship between the UK and the EU might evolve in the future. The key questions this book seeks to explore are as follows:

How have the patterns in the British discourse on Europe evolved in terms of changes and continuities across the 1975 referendum debates, the Maastricht debates of the 1990s, and proto-referendum debates of the 2013?

What are the implications and effects of these changes and continuities, and in particular the increasing importance of immigration in the discourse, likely to be for the forthcoming referendum debate?

1.3   Book Outline

This study proceeds in a well-recognised form and therefore begins in earnest with a chapter setting out the foundational detail of theory and methodology. The chapter outlines the ontological and epistemological assumptions that underpin my discourse-analytical approach. I discuss a number of key concepts here, including the interaction of truth, knowledge, authority, and power, with reference to Bartelson (Bartelson 1995) and Foucault (1980). Neumann's work on self and other (Neumann 1999) is also of major importance here. In terms of the method for the study, the book draws upon Lene Hansen's highly useful guide in the first half of *Security as practice: discourse analysis and the Bosnian war* (Hansen 2006). The sources for analysis are drawn from political speeches, campaign literature, and newspaper editorials. A number of analytical tools are presented, including linking and differentiation, and intertextuality. The chapter concludes with some brief reflections on limitations and author bias.

The book focuses on three particular peaks in the discourse: the 1975 referendum campaign, the Treaty of Maastricht ratification debates of 1992–1993, and the proto-referendum debates of 2013. This episodic approach is useful in delivering a manageable amount of source material.

Why are these three periods relevant? Taking each in turn, the previous referendum campaign is clearly of interest given the prospect of another campaign in 2017. The campaign's oppositional nature presents a good opportunity to analyse different constructions of identity. The second peak of the Maastricht debates has become notorious in British politics for the frenetic nature of its discourse and the related destruction of the authority of Prime Minister John Major. It demonstrates that the discourse on Europe had had major implications for the fortunes of Prime Ministers and political parties in the UK. The third peak, the proto-referendum debates of 2013, keeps us updated and allows us to finish our "history of the present in terms of the past" (Bartelson 1995:7–8). This peak is also notable in that the Prime Minister found his range of options narrowed to the point of being forced into a referendum commitment he initially wanted to avoid (see Cameron 2012).

The three discursive peaks each receive a chapter of analysis, meaning one chapter each on 1975, 1992–1993, and 2013. These chapters begin with an overview of the sources used, how the chapter relates to the book's research questions, and a summary of the representations uncovered in the discourse. A brief bit of historical/political context is then provided before the detail of each major and minor representation is set out. The final chapter concludes the study by drawing out the key continuities and key changes across the 40-year period under analysis. I also use this conclusion to assess the likely effects and implications of these continuities and changes for the referendum campaign.

NOTE

1. David Cameron's fairly reasonable justification against a referendum was that the Lisbon Treaty had already been ratified before he came to power.

REFERENCES

Bartelson, J. (1995). *A genealogy of sovereignty.* Cambridge studies in international relations. Cambridge: Cambridge University Press. x, 317 p. pp.

Cameron, D. (2012, June 30). David Cameron: We need to be clear about the best way of getting what is best for Britain. *The Daily Telegraph.*

Cameron, D. (2013). David Cameron's speech on the EU: Full text. *The New Statesman.* Retrieved January 10, 2013, from http://www.newstatesman.com/politics/2013/01/david-camerons-speech-eu-full-text

Carey, S., & Geddes, A. (2010). Less is more: Immigration and European integration at the 2010 General Election. *Parliamentary Affairs, 63*(4), 849–865.

Daddow, O. (2006). Euroscepticism and the culture of the discipline of history. *Review of International Studies, 32*(2), 309–328.

Foucault, M. & Gordon, C. (1980). Power/knowledge: selected interviews and other writings, 1972–1977. Brighton: Harvester. xi, 270 p. pp.

George, S. (1998). *An awkward partner: Britain in the European community.* Oxford: Oxford University Press.

Hansen, L. (2006). *Security as practice: Discourse analysis and the Bosnian war.* London: Routledge. xxiii, 259 p. pp.

Mason, R. (2013, 29 May). 'Tories more divided' under David Cameron than John Major. *The Telegraph.*

Montgomerie, T. (2012). 100 Tory MPs call for Cameron to prepare legislation for EU referendum. ConservativeHome.Retrieved May 12, from http://www.conservativehome.com/thetorydiary/2012/06/100-tory-mps-call-for-cameron-to-prepare-legislation-for-eu-referendum.html

Neumann, I. B. (1999). *Uses of the other: "The East" in European identity formation.* Manchester: Manchester University Press. xv, 281 p. pp.

Spiering, M. (2004). British Euroscepticism. *European Studies: A Journal of European Culture, History and Politics, 20*(1), 127–149.

Watt, N. (2013, April 24). UKIP's popularity will hit Tories hardest, says professor. *The Guardian.*

YouGov. (2014). YouGov/Sunday Times survey results. Retrieved April 28, from http://d25d2506sfb94s.cloudfront.net/cumulus_uploads/document/pjvdg1r9fz/YG-Archive-Pol-Sunday-Times-results-140525.pdf

YouGov. (2015). YouGov survey results. YouGov Cambridge, Europe. Retrieved January 12, from https://d25d2506sfb94s.cloudfront.net/cumulus_uploads/document/1d6iphzuzx/EUResults_November2015-WebsiteV2.pdf

CHAPTER 2

Theory and Methodology

Abstract The chapter provides a clear, concise, and accessible introduction to discourse analysis. It describes the work's key underlying theoretical assumptions and overall approach before details of the method are explained. The chapter introduces Parliamentary debates, newspaper editorials, and keynote political speeches as empirical sources, as well as a range of relevant analytical techniques.

Keywords Identity • Foreign policy • Discourse analysis • Self and other • Positions, themes, and representations

It is often said that learning begins with the "three 'R's" of reading, writing, and arithmetic. I shall modify this tradition by beginning not with the three 'R's but, rather, with the two 'R's of rationalism and reflectivism. These two positions within the field of International Relations, so categorised in Robert Keohane's seminal 1988 address to the International Studies Association (Keohane 1988), are characterised by very different ontological and epistemological viewpoints. Rationalism is associated with objectivist ontology and positivist epistemology. Reflectivism meanwhile eschews a causal epistemology, focusing instead on interpretivist processes of mutual constitution and change. This study is conducted from a reflectivist standpoint. To be more specific, it takes a poststructuralist approach to examining the relationship between the UK and the rest of the EU. Using poststructuralist dis-

© The Editor(s) (if applicable) and The Author(s) 2016
J. Todd, *The UK's Relationship with Europe*,
DOI 10.1007/978-3-319-33669-5_2

course analysis provides a historically informed yet contemporarily relevant understanding of how David Cameron's referendum commitment became possible, and enables us to propose some implications for the referendum campaign itself.

2.1   ONTOLOGY

A poststructuralist approach implies certain ontological and epistemological assumptions. The two are bound closely together—my view of how the world *is* directly influences the ways in which I access and investigate it. This process works, of course, in the other direction as well—how I investigate the world will affect my understanding of it. Neumann completes this circle:

> Nietzsche stressed that the world does not simply present itself to human beings, but that the activity of knowing is a formulation of the world. This knowing cannot take place from any solid foundation, and so the self will know the other and everything else only as a series of changing perspectives, not as a foundational fact. Indeed, it is the knowing that makes the self, not the other way around. (Neumann 1999:12)

Given that ontology and epistemology are so closely bound together, it is slightly problematic to begin with one and then proceed to the other without implying causality. As Walker says, "it is not always easy to begin at the beginning, if only because the point of origin depends on where we are now" (Walker 1989:26).

I follow a poststructuralist ontology as described by Lene Hansen (2006:1): "The relationship between identity and foreign policy is at the centre of poststructuralism's research agenda." Hansen argues that foreign policies are based on representations of identity, but identities are also produced and reproduced through foreign policy (see also Campbell 1998). As Gaskarth (2006:327) notes, "in describing or performing an activity linguistically, we are producing its meaning and so creating, reinforcing, or changing policy understanding and practice." Poststructuralists like Hansen thus understand the relationship between identity and foreign policy as mutually constitutive rather than causal (ibid.:xvi, 5) (Fig. 2.1):

Fig. 2.1 The constitutive relationship between identity and foreign policy

To unpack this a little, it may be helpful to use an example. When British political leaders argue that the UK is different from other EU members and therefore requires a different deal (e.g. opting out of Schengen), we can observe both a foreign policy based on this sense of difference *and* this sense of difference being reproduced and reinforced.

That identity and foreign policy are mutually constitutive is an ontological viewpoint supported by a range of poststructuralist thinkers including Der Derian, Shapiro, and Neumann. Der Derian (1989:4) argues that discourses construct, not just reflect reality, whilst Shapiro (1989:14) posits that "representations are not descriptions of a world of facticity, but are ways of making facticity." There may be those reading this who cry out objections that "these are all just words" and what really matters are the things you can measure and count, be it aircraft carriers, GDP, or polling numbers. I would argue in response that identity is an essential mediator of how such numbers are interpreted, particularly in a foreign policy context. As Wendt's classic example regarding nuclear weapons explains: "500 British nuclear weapons are less threatening to the United States than 5 North Korean nuclear weapons, because the British are friends of the United States and the North Koreans are not." (Wendt 1995:73)

The identity–foreign policy nexus demands consideration of self and other because "delineation of a self from an other is an active and ongoing part of identity formation" (Neumann 1999:35). Connolly (1989:329) puts it simply that "Identity and difference are bound together." It is worth noting that, whilst these processes of identity formation may occur at both an individual and a collective level, our interest is in the collective. Such collective selves could be a group of football fans bound together by a dislike of their local rivals, a hegemonic state railing against an "Axis of Evil," or even a multistate grouping such as Europe "constituted against the temporal Other of its own violent past" (Wæver 1996 cited in Hansen 2006:40). The framing and representation of self and other are therefore important. Græger (2005:86) notes that those who control how an issue is framed also control, to a great extent, how that issue is managed. As mentioned in the Introduction, if an issue like migration is consistently framed as a security threat, this will likely invoke a different range of policy responses than if it was framed as an economic opportunity.

To sum this up, these ontological positions speak to a research agenda which engages with how those in positions of power (be it politicians, the media, or others) seek to make or influence policy on the basis of identity representations. It is important to note that collective identities are multifaceted and should be studied as such (Neumann 1999:30, 36). Just as there are many interpretations of what it means to be British, German, or European, there are many interpretations of how questions of foreign policy should be answered—and both of these are contested (ibid.:30). This suggests we should be cautious in assuming an over-simplified self/other dichotomy. Not only are collective identities multifaceted, but the other can, depending on how identity is constructed, be somewhere on a spectrum of different degrees of "Otherness"(Hansen 2006:7). Issues may not always be represented as a Manichean battle between a good self and evil other.

2.2   Methodology

This section justifies my poststructuralist approach to discourse analysis with an explanation of the epistemological assumptions bound up in the ontological viewpoint mentioned earlier. In building my methodology, I shall therefore discuss the interaction of four phenomena with the identity–foreign policy nexus. These phenomena are truth, knowledge, authority, and power. I will examine each of these phenomena in turn, though it is important to note that this should not imply a causal chain. Rather, these phenomena affect identity and foreign policy in a mutually reinforcing manner.

Beginning with *truth*, Foucault (in Rabinow 1991:74) and Bartelson (1995:2) affirm that discourses are a battle over truth and that analysing discourse is therefore an attempt to "understand clashes between different version of political truth" (ibid.:4). This seems particularly appropriate when considering how best to analyse the highly contested political relationship between the UK and the EU. The close link between truth and *knowledge* is described by Jørgensen et al.(2002:13), who assert that truth is a discursive construction, with different regimes of knowledge determining what is true and false. Bartelson follows this logic, noting that knowledge provides a system for the formation of valid statements and that therefore "all knowledge is knowledge by differentiation, and this differentiation is a political activity" (Bartelson 1995:6). The political act of differentiation is also described by Neumann (1999:140), who notes that political actors use differentiation to serve political causes and that this differentiation is in itself a political act. Those studying ethnic conflict have similarly observed the importance of social construction of identities linked to violence (see, e.g. Fearon and Laitin 2000).

Political actors need *authority* to carry out this differentiation. Buzan et al. (1998:33) note that such actors require a position of authority in order to have the necessary social capital to convince their audience. Hansen (2006:8) makes a link between authority and knowledge, in that policymakers gain their authority *both* from their position in government and from their knowledge about a given issue. Governments not only have legislative authority (i.e. the ability to make laws), but also a large amount of day-to-day authority and ability to frame issues and make decisions (although in a democracy this authority is not absolute). This shows how the notion of authority is closely bound to that of *power*. Foucault argues that power is not only repressive, but is also productive in that it forms knowledge and produces discourse: "it needs to be considered as a productive network which runs through the social body, much more than as a negative instance whose function is repression." (Foucault and Gordon 1980:119). Power, in Foucault's view, is therefore not merely the ability to impose one's will on another; it also acts in more subtle, less tangible ways in that it defines what we think of as feasible, natural— indeed, what we understand as true or false. Consider here, who in the UK has the power to shape citizens' knowledge and understanding of the Eurozone crisis; who was to blame, how should it be solved, and to what extent should the UK be involved? Foucault relates power to truth as follows: truth "is to be understood as a system of ordered procedures for the production, regulation, distribution, circulation and operation of statements... [and] is linked in a circular relation with systems of power which produce and sustain it, and to effects of power which it induces and which extend it" (Foucault and Gordon 1980:133). So the battle over truth, rather than being about uncovering some objective and absolute truth ("the fact of the matter," as politicians are wont to describe their version of it), is a power-infused struggle not just to win the argument at hand, but to set the rules for current and future arguments. The four phenomena of truth, knowledge, authority, and power therefore have important consequences for identity and foreign policy (Fig. 2.2):

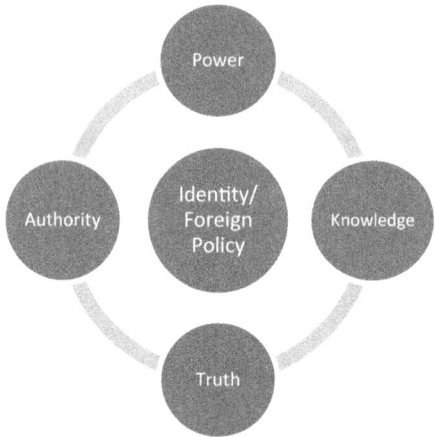

Fig. 2.2   Power, authority, truth, and knowledge

These phenomena can be accessed and analysed through discourse. Jørgensen and Phillips note that discourse analysis is an appropriate framework for the analysis of national identity (2002:2). Wæver invokes Anderson's imagined communities, asserting that the discursive and symbolic construction of political identity means that we can investigate "how the nation/state identification is upheld by way of narratives on Europe" (Wæver 2002:25). Neumann also argues the need to focus on "how social boundaries between human collectives are maintained" and that "[w]hen studying the self/other nexus, the starting point should be to identify the slash and how it is maintained" (Neumann 1999:5, 36). This slash sits between the self and other, forming a boundary between Neumann's human collectives. Ashley (1989:285) supports this, affirming that poststructuralist studies should analyse the "nonplace" that sits between the international and the domestic. The relationship between the UK and the EU is, in my view, a highly apposite case, in that the various positions on EU membership are essentially debates on where this "slash" between a British self and Continental other is placed.

So far this section has provided a general, high-level justification for using poststructuralist discourse analysis for studying the UK–EU relationship. I shall now develop a more specific rationale with reference to my research questions.

2.3   RESEARCH QUESTIONS

How have the patterns in the British discourse on Europe evolved in terms of changes and continuities across the 1975 referendum debates, the Maastricht debates of the 1990s, and proto-referendum debates of the 2013?

What are the implications and effects of these changes and continuities, and in particular the increasing importance of immigration in the discourse, likely to be for the referendum debate?

With a focus on identity and foreign policy, it is important to analyse the discourse over time, examining discursive changes and continuities. This genealogical approach, famously expounded by Foucault and Bartelson, is "a history of the present in terms of its past" that enables us to understand "how the present became logically possible" (Bartelson 1995:7–8). Bartelson quotes Nietzsche's affirmation "that the historian's history always has more to do with the present than with the past" (ibid.:54). I would argue that this phenomenon is even more acute when we consider a *politician's* version of history. Ashley (1989:283) propounds a similarly historical approach, urging the need to investigate the processes of how meaning (i.e. knowledge) is imposed and reinterpreted. The assertion that "Very few politicians and diplomats, and only the most ardent positivist scholars, would probably object to the genealogical presupposition that the way a political question has been variously discussed in the past will impinge upon the political business at hand" (Neumann 1999:66) is also worth presenting here. Bartelson (1995:7–8) affirms that this genealogical approach has two key implications for method: that such studies must be episodic and that they should be exemplary in nature. I will return to these implications in the Methods section later in the text. Bartelson (ibid.:52–3) focuses his work on sovereignty, which he conceptualises as a parergon, or frame, between the domestic and international, between anarchy and hierarchy. There is a clear link here to self/other, with Bartelson's concept of sovereignty representing the "slash" prioritised by Neumann and Ashley.

In terms of looking specifically at the position of immigration within the British discourse on Europe, representations regarding immigration are focused on the internal other or a prospective internal other. As Connolly (1989:326) states, "[T]he definition of the internal other and the external other compound one another." With reference to Wæver and Hansen,

Neumann (1999:30) argues that "In Europe, friction between leaders and polities on issues of migration and EU integration may be seen to reveal contending conceptions of security, where the states' insistence on the pooling of sovereignty clashes with the societies' insistence on maintaining the borders between ethnically defined nations." Since Neumann made this observation in the 1990s, populist parties across Europe have, of course, successfully both exploited and reproduced this friction.

2.4   RELEVANT LITERATURE

This section cannot, in the space available, hope to provide a comprehensive picture of all that has been written about UK–EU relations. However, there are a number of key contributions against whose theoretical, methodological, and empirical insights this work must position itself.

Henrik Larsen published two works in the late 1990s that drew inspiration from the thinking of Ole Wæver and others from the Copenhagen School (Larsen 1997, 1999). Both take a discursive approach to European policies of states, including the UK, with Larsen arguing that discourse is both embedded in, and shapes, a social context. Larsen notes the salience of parliamentary sovereignty as a nodal point in the discourse (1999:476): the enduring importance of this concept is borne out by this book (see also Braun 2008). That said, I have sympathy with Diez's (1997) critique in his review of Larsen's book. In particular, Diez highlights Larsen's separation of discourse from policy and lack of attention to economics: these are in my view fair criticisms. Also, Larsen's (1999:454) delineation between "expressions of discourse" and "purely rhetorical/tactical uses of language" is somewhat questionable, particularly given his assertion that discourse analysis is not about studying views as mental states in individuals. Diez's (2001) important conceptualisation of Europe as a discursive battleground must also be addressed here. Diez argues that European policy articulations are drawn from (and reproduce) larger discourses (he terms them "metanarratives"): these might be historical or market-based discourses, for example. My approach of identifying key themes in the discourse (e.g. economic issues) is a slightly different way of linking in these larger discourses. I agree with Diez's argument that it is important to retain the ability to focus on issues of interest to traditional policy analysis, even if beginning from a different theoretical starting point. In seeking to solve the thorny issue of prioritising either agent or structure, Diez introduces the Discursive Nodal Points as key concepts that are discursively contested via different articulations. In later work, Diez develops this notion of contestation by focusing on discursive struggles and how they delimit policy outcomes (see Diez 2014). I find this approach to be of greater salience when looking at a single state and its relationship with the EU.

Another milestone text is Medrano's work *Framing Europe* (2003). Whilst not taking precisely the same theoretical or methodological starting point as this work (his use of framing is more cognitive than discursive), Medrano's analysis of how people and elites frame European integration is nonetheless relevant. For example, he highlights that his British informants "conceived [the EU] as a sort of superstate gobbling up British sovereignty and identity" (p.68, 215). Medrano also writes convincingly about the cultural embeddedness of a sense of difference from "the Continent." His analysis of newspaper sources is also noteworthy, though he focuses on two smaller-circulation weekly newspapers—"the intelligentsia's printed legacy" (p.106)—rather than the mass-market papers analysed in this book.

Huysmans (2006) provides another useful example of how the thinking of the Copenhagen School can be brought to bear on the issue of European integration. Huysmans focuses in particular on the security framing of the issues of migration, asylum, and refugee policy. The arguments about the politicisation of migration and asylum are of relevance to this work and its interest in the rising prominence of immigration issues within the debates on EU membership (see also Ford et al. 2012).

Daddow (2011) gives a comprehensive account of Tony Blair and Gordon Brown's ultimately unsuccessful discursive endeavour against the orthodox us/them narrative that is hegemonic in the British discourse on Europe. Daddow's work is relevant to this book, theoretically and methodologically, in that it combines discourse analysis with Finnemore and Sikkink's (1998) concept of norm entrepreneurship. Whilst this approach has value (particularly when focusing in on two key actors in Prime Ministers Blair and Brown), I believe an approach focusing on themes and representations in the discourse is appealing in its relative methodological asceticism. In addition, it avoids any potential problems with analysing change as highlighted by Hofferberth and Weber (2015). Daddow's work is also useful given his account of the academic quest to define Euroscepticism. I share his concerns about the empirical applicability of Kopecý and Mudde's (2002) four categories of Euro-enthusiasts, pragmatists, sceptics, and rejects. Daddow also notes that the categorisation of Euroscepticism as either hard (i.e. principled opposition to EU membership) or soft (qualified opposition to aspects of EU membership) of Taggart and Szczerbiak (2001,2002) is open to criticism for being overly broad. Nonetheless, it is this categorisation that is most widely used and is the one to which I return in this work.

De Wilde and Trenz (2012) explore Euroscepticism as an element of discourse, observing that "different actors compete for the hegemony of their readings of the EU" (p. 13). The authors argue in favour of a focus on mass media, which I agree is essential. This work nonetheless takes in political speeches of both government and opposition figures, as such speeches are another important part of the discourse given these actors' authority and agenda-setting potential.

Gibbins (2014) seeks to shed light on British national identity through analysing "the various perceptions British political elites have had of Europe" (p. 4). The book examines how different conceptions of Europe are represented by different "others," be it friendly, non-radical, or radical othering. Gibbins' work addresses both the 1975 referendum and the Maastricht debates (in addition to the Treaty of Lisbon), and here his analysis chimes, to a certain, degree with this work (he highlights, for example, references to sovereignty and democracy). However, Gibbins' book does not substantively address the increasing prominence of immigration.

With regard to Euroscepticism in the UK, Gifford (2014a:13) argues that it has become systemic, indeed "central to the reproduction of a distinct and exceptional British state." Gifford has also argued that the embeddedness of hard Euroscepticism constrains governing autonomy regarding Europe (Gifford 2014b). Spiering's (2014) *A Cultural History of British Euroscepticism* underlines the deep roots of the Anglo-European cultural divide. Similarly, Vasilopoulou (2013:154) argues that whilst the term Euroscepticism might have been coined in the 1980s, "its features were present from the early stages of the European integration process." This deep-rootedness can be observed in the Eurosceptic calls to history set out in the empirical chapters that follow.

The work edited by Tournier-Sol and Gifford (2015) describes Euroscepticism as "a systemic and determining feature not only of the UK and the EU but also of UK political society more broadly" (location 176). The book addresses four key themes: the nation and national identity, the Euroscepticism of political parties, Euroscepticism in civil society, and the strategic interests of the British state. This work adds, in particular, to the first and second of these themes. The chapters by Crowley, Alexandre-Collier, Tournier-Sol, Daddow and Macmillan are therefore of relevance, and I will return to them in the empirical chapters. Baker and Schnapper's (2015) analysis of the effect of the Eurozone crisis on the UK, EU, and their relationship observes the increasing entrenchment of Euroscepticism and asserts that the aggressive attitude of British elites in response to the Eurozone crisis increases the risks of a Brexit.

The recent special issue of the *Journal of Common Market Studies* entitled *Interpreting British European Policy* adopts an interpretivist perspective to analyse the current state of play regarding the UK's relationship with Europe. This interpretivist approach chimes nicely with the perspective adopted in this work (see also Bevir and Daddow 2015). The introductory article highlights the importance of "historically informed narrative traditions as background influences on policy decision-making" (Bevir et al. 2015:5). I agree with the authors that it is important to look beyond elite discourse as purely a rationalist tool of party competition. This work picks up a number of themes and issues from the Special Issue. Ludlow's (2015) article on the EC membership debate of 1971 provides useful context to the chapter on the 1975 referendum, showing that concerns about parliamentary sovereignty were expressed even at this stage. Kenny (2015) describes the return of "Englishness" and its implications for the UK–EU relationship. He observes the increasing prominence of a populist-nationalist narrative, evoked by tabloid newspapers, media pundits, Conservative MPs, and, in particular, UKIP.

The edited volume *Britain's Future in Europe: Reform, renegotiation, repatriation or secession?* (Emerson et al. 2015) is an analysis of the British government's review of EU competences. The volume's different empirical focus (policy fields like the single market and justice and home affairs) means that this book provides a distinct perspective on UK–EU relations. Liddle's (2014) *The Europe Dilemma: Britain and the Drama of EU Integration* is also relevant, though it focuses primarily on Labour's term of office from 1997 to 2010. Seldon and Snowdon's (2015) insider-style account of David Cameron's first term as Prime Minister includes relevant sections on UK–EU relations and immigration, including a quotation from Cameron that the British "problem" with Europe goes to "the very heart of the British understanding of democracy" (cited at location 4506).

All in all, this work seeks to build on the aforementioned literature, adding value through its focus on three key periods and its inclusion of the increasingly febrile debates around immigration.

2.5   METHOD

I begin this section with a brief observation about the difference between methodology and method: "Methods mediate between research questions and the answers which data partially provide to them; methodology justifies and guarantees that process of mediation" (Clough and Nutbrown 2002:38). So, having made the case for the overall approach, this section gets down to the nuts and bolts of how the analysis will be delivered. There are three key steps to explain:

1. How to delimit and select texts
2. How to read and analyse the relevant texts
3. How to map and layer representations.

2.5.1   Delimiting and Selecting Texts

Hansen proposes four research models for delimiting texts (2006:64). I have selected a Model 2 study as the most appropriate: this model includes official government discourse as well as the political opposition and media. Given the contested nature of the discourse on Europe in the UK, including the opposition and media in the analysis is essential. Hansen (2006:61) notes that parliamentary debates are useful in that they are oppositional and public; this means they are particularly appropriate for a highly contested issue like the UK's relationship with Europe. One of the key challenges with text delimitation and selection is acquiring "enough" without becoming overwhelmed. Bartelson's episodic approach is helpful here. Similarly, Hansen suggests "selection of texts to a timeline that identifies periods of higher levels of political and media activity," because this "provides a structure for an analysis of change" (ibid.:87). This study therefore focuses on three peaks in the discourse (both in terms of level of activity and intensity of the debate): the 1975 referendum on European Economic Community (EEC) membership, the Maastricht Treaty debates in the early 1990s, and the proto-referendum debates in the aftermath of Cameron's referendum commitment. Each of these episodes is addressed in a separate chapter of analysis. With regard to selecting individual texts that are exemplary, Hansen notes that texts should contain clear articulation of identities and policies, be widely read and attended to, and have formal authority to define a political position (ibid.:85). Hansen's final point regarding formal authority is one I would broaden to *effective authority.* Whilst Hansen later accepts that formal political authority is "by definition irrelevant" (ibid.:86) when considering media texts, I argue that considering effective authority is more useful, particularly in a context where "the *Daily Mail* factor" is an acknowledged part of the political landscape.

In terms of testing whether the elusive "enough" has been achieved, Neumann (2008:69–70) acknowledges that Foucault's assertion to "read everything, study everything" is, in practice, unfeasible and that "relatively few texts will constitute the main points of reference." Dunn (2008:90) notes the requirement to make "tough decisions" in order to make a project "doable." Essentially, I shall seek to analyse enough sources to build a convincing set of themes and representations without overlooking any key texts.

The details of the sources selected for each of the three episodes (1970s, 1990s, and current) are set out in Table 2.1. In broad terms, the key political speeches (particularly parliamentary debates) and newspaper editorials will be analysed. Editorials provide a useful proxy for the overall tone and content of a given newspaper's coverage of an issue. If Europe features in an editorial, it will also receive significant coverage elsewhere in the paper.

In addition to the specific sources for each episode, I have selected two general histories of the period to provide "historical material that traces the genealogy of the dominant representations" (Hansen 2006:82). The first is *This Blessed Plot* by Hugo Young (1998), which is written from a pro-Europe perspective. The second is *The Great Deception: Can the European Union Survive?* by Christopher Booker and Richard North (2005); it is written from a Eurosceptic perspective.

2.5.2   *Reading and Analysis*

Moving to reading and analysis, there are a number of techniques to employ. First, Hansen (2006:41–2) states that it is important to begin with "identifying those terms that indicate a clear construction of the Other ... or of the Self." Hansen brings in Derrida's view of language privileging one element over its opposite in a series of juxtapositions to propose two processes that work together to construct identity: a positive process of linking and a negative process of differentiation (ibid.:19, see also Tajfel and Turner 1986). For example, a far-right political party might link together positive aspects of a "Native British" self, such as "brave," "independent," and "democratic," and differentiate them negatively with an other constituted of "foreigners," "asylum

Table 2.1 Overview of empirical sources

Sources	Timeframe	Notes
1975		
The Parliamentary debate on the *White Paper on the Membership of the European Community.*	April 1975	The White Paper debate focused on the arguments for and against membership. The later debates on the Referendum Act 1975 focused on the nuts and bolts of holding a referendum.
Key referendum campaign literature.	1975	Three main leaflets were produced—a Government leaflet, a "Yes" campaign leaflet, and a "No" campaign leaflet.
Editorials mentioning the referendum and/or the EEC from *The Times,* the *Daily Express,* and the *Daily Mirror.*	January–December 1975	*The Times* is included because of its status as the UK "paper of record." The other three papers had the highest circulation figures at the time and represent different political positions.
1992–1993		
Parliamentary debates on the European Communities (Amendment) Act 1993, which enabled the ratification of the Maastricht Treaty and the subsequent debates on the Social Protocol.	May 1992–July 1993	The debates on the Social Protocol were a key moment in the Maastricht "rebellion" and are therefore included in the analysis.
Editorials mentioning the Maastricht Treaty and/or the EEC from *The Times* and the *Daily Mail.*	May 1992–July 1993	The *Daily Mail* has replaced the *Daily Express* for this episode because it had higher circulation figures and greater political influence.
2013		
Parliamentary debates on the European Union (Referendum) Bill.	July–December 2013	This is a Private Members Bill (i.e. not a Government Bill) because the referendum commitment is not Government policy.
David Cameron's referendum speech	January 2013	This was a key speech given outside Parliament.
UKIP leader Nigel Farage's party conference speech.	September 2013	The UKIP leader is not an MP and so does not feature in the Parliamentary debates. However, he is an important figure in the EU debate.
Editorials mentioning the referendum and/or the EU from *The Times, The Sun,* the *Daily Mail* and the *Daily Mirror.*	January–December 2013	Given the Parliamentary debates are shorter for 2013, *The Sun* has been added to the range of newspapers analysed.

seekers," "immigrants," and "Muslim extremism."[1] This process of differentiation is also prioritised by Walker (1995:328), who asserts that "structural patterns are constituted through historical processes of differentiation." Hansen presents these processes of linking and differentiation graphically. Figure 2.3 is an example of the Islamic and Danish representations constructed in the wake of the Danish cartoon crisis (Hansen 2007:11).

In addition to these processes of linking and differentiation, Hansen (2006:46) asserts the importance of spatiality, temporality, and ethicality as "analytical lenses that bring out the important political substance of identity construction." Spatial dimensions of identity might include specific countries or regions (e.g. the rest of Europe being termed "the continent" as viewed from the UK). Temporal dimensions often contrast progress and development with backwardness and intransigence. Finally, ethical dimensions of identity might include moral judgements on issues of criminality or lower standards of democracy. I consider that it is helpful to view these identities as potentially overlapping, in that a given representation can address more than one of the three dimensions (see Fig. 2.3). For example, Nigel Farage often refers to "criminal Romanian gangs," a representation which takes in both ethical and spatial dimensions.

The final reading technique to be employed is intertextuality, that is, when "one spoken or written text alludes to, quotes, or otherwise relates to another one" (Gee 2011:208). Bakhtin proposes a circularity of effect

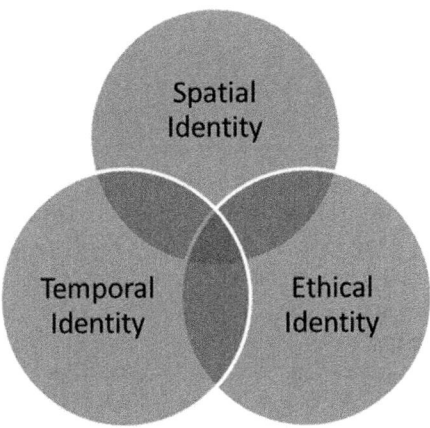

Fig. 2.3   The spatial, temporal, and ethical dimensions of identity

and meaning between new texts and those that precede them (see Bakhtin et al. 1981). Hansen (2006:8) draws on this to state that intertextuality is a method to build both arguments and authority. She goes on to affirm that foreign policy texts "all strive to establish themselves as having the authority to speak about a particular foreign policy issue" (ibid.:66). This applies more generally as well: a simple example from the spoken word would be a religious leader building a sermon around quotations from the Bible or the Quran. Hansen describes intertextuality as having two types: explicit and implicit (or conceptual) intertextuality. Explicit intertextuality involves direct quoting from previous texts (quoting Churchill would be a common example in the British political discourse). Implicit/conceptual intertextuality relies on common understandings and catchphrases that tap into a body of knowledge built up over time. A related example here would be references to the UK as an "island nation" or "these islands," which draw, via Churchillian-inspired rhetoric, on wartime memories and emotions. Although not referring explicitly to intertextuality, Gaskarth (2006:328) notes that "invoking great statesmen of the past" helps build authority.

Each of these analytical techniques will be employed to assess the sources for linking and differentiation; spatial, temporal, and ethical dimensions of identity; and intertextuality.

2.5.3   Mapping and Layering: Positions, Themes, and Representations

The aforementioned techniques enable significant analytical detail to be produced from the sources. This detail needs to be assembled in such a way to provide a picture of the discourse at a given time. The first step is to identify what Neumann terms "*positions*"[2] (2008:71), where "[t]ypically, one position will be dominant, and one or two other positions will challenge it on certain points." With regard to the subject at hand, it is straightforward to imagine at least two positions being present: pro- and anti-Europe. That being said, the discourse might well be more open than that, with—for example—"hard" and "soft" Eurosceptic positions present (see Taggart and Szczerbiak 2001).

With a topic as broad and overarching as the UK's relationship to Europe, the discourse of course can be broken down into a number of major and minor *themes*. Whilst many analyses move directly from identifying positions to mapping representations, I consider it helpful to first set out what was being discussed, be it the economic implications of EEC/EU membership, or the prospects for parliamentary sovereignty. These themes are sites of contestation within the discourse, as actors seek to frame, or represent, issues in a certain way. Sometimes one position's representations of an issue will dominate a particular theme (e.g. hard Eurosceptic representations dominate when looking at the theme of immigration in the discourse of 2013). This use of themes might open up the analysis to criticism for being merely descriptive, but I believe there is merit in showing how the discourse has evolved in terms of positions (e.g. pro- and anti-Europe), themes (e.g. economy, immigration, sovereignty), and representations (e.g. the EU as a threat to British democracy). These three stages can be labelled as "who," "what," and "how," respectively, enabling the analysis to show clearly both the issues at hand and how they are represented by those occupying the various positions in the discourse.

When mapping out a coherent and comprehensive set of *representations* (Hansen notes that such representations might be "geographical identities, historical analogies, striking metaphors, or political concepts" (2006:53)), it is useful to begin with a small number of key texts. These might be Prime Ministerial speeches, government policy documents, and/or opposition responses. Starting with these enables a provisional set of positions to be sketched out. More detailed analysis of the discourse will then substantiate or disqualify each provisional representation. The three campaign documents (Government, "Yes," and "No") are a useful example of key texts that can be used to achieve this for 1975.

Layering of the discourse can take a number of forms, although this study will focus on two methods: assessing the dominant/marginal nature of the positions in the discourse and assessing change in the themes and representations over time. The first of these layering techniques is important because "political practices are permeated by dominant discourses that shape subjectivity and constitute meaningful objects" (Fournier 2012:27). Similarly, "any actual historical reconstruction is likely to proceed by marginalisation; that which looks obscure, absurd or patently false from the viewpoint of our present is systematically subdued, and only that which chimes well with modern knowledge is admitted to the narrative core" (Bartelson 1995:68). There is a link here to Græger's (2005) concept of framing, in that those enjoying a dominant position will be able to frame an issue on their terms. Given the scope of my research questions, assessing change over time is clearly an essential element of this study, hence its structure of an analytical chapter on each of the key episodes (1970s, 1990s and 2013).

2.6   Reflections on Potential Limitations and Bias

The previous sections set out in detail the choices I have made to define my approach to this study. All such decisions have strengths and weaknesses. The rationale underpinning the strengths of my approach should, at this point, be clear. However, it is important to assess the potential weaknesses inherent in my approach as well. Beginning with my overall reflectivist approach, the rejection of an objectivist "view from nowhere" means that I must consider author bias. Bias is very difficult—indeed most likely impossible—to avoid, since "The discourse analyst is often anchored in exactly the same discourses as he or she wants to analyse" (Jørgensen et al. 2002:49). The first objective with regard to bias should be to avoid fulfilling Wight's (1995:27) lament that "The conviction usually precedes the evidence." With regard to how to position ourselves when analysing discourse, Bartelson (1995:5) proposes that we should "situate ourselves as detached spectators within history." This concept of being within the discourse, but detached, helps answer Leander's call for "epistemological prudence," whereby one seeks to limit the impact of one's bias and maintain awareness of it when analysing results. Dunn goes further, stating that "I do not believe it is possible to strive for some mythical goal of objectivity, since no such terra firma exists. Therefore, I recognize I am not neutral, and I am not too concerned with charges of interpretative bias" (Dunn 2008:91). I *am* somewhat concerned about interpretive bias and its implications for validity, so I should set out my position and background.

I grew up in Northern Ireland on a diet of UK news and current affairs and worked in the civil service in Belfast and London for nearly a decade, spending much of my career in close contact with Government Ministers and the Houses of Parliament. These experiences gave me a good degree of what Neumann (2008:63) terms "cultural competence." I know the political landscape of the UK well, including how both news and policy are produced. On the contrary, my political views (generally, if at times, frustratedly, pro-Europe) will, to some degree, have an impact on my analysis. To maximise the validity of this study, I will need to manage these views.

There are a number of further potential issues to address that fall outside the scope of the five tests. The first is regarding my decisions on the scope of this study. The scope could be criticised from a genealogical perspective as being too limited: a history of the present in terms of the past should, perhaps, stretch for more than 40 years. On the contrary, given that this is a concise book, there is also a risk that the scope is too broad and thus any analysis will be superficial. However, narrowing the scope of analysis to three peaks in the discourse provides a good deal of detail. It is also important to consider if other important periods should have been included, for example, the entry debates in 1971, the 1987 Single European Act, or the ratification of the Treaty of Lisbon in 2008. These three periods are undoubtedly also important, but I contend that the Maastricht ratification debates and the proto-referendum debates are of greater importance (and more highly contested) than the Single European Act and Lisbon treaty debates, respectively. The entry debates are, of course, of foundational importance to the UK's relationship with the EU, but given this book was inspired by David Camron's referendum commitment, it made sense to analyse the previous referendum campaign.

2.7   Chapter Conclusion

This chapter has sought to set out how, in ontological and epistemological terms, a poststructuralist discourse-analytical approach can give useful insights that other theories, such as more rationalist approaches, cannot, in relation to the specifics of this study's research questions. Of particular importance to the study of the British discourse on Europe are the notions that identity and foreign policy are mutually constitutive and that differentiation between self and other is an essential part of identity formation. Regarding method, the oppositional nature of the British discourse on Europe means that parliamentary debates and newspaper editorials fall within the study's scope. A number of relevant analytical tools that enable the study of self/other delineation in identity formation are introduced. These are linking and differentiation, different dimensions of identity (spatial, temporal, and ethical) and intertextuality. Each of these tools is used in the empirical chapters that follow. Finally, the chapter provided a reflection on how my own position and biases might affect this study. Having established theory and method, the way is therefore clear for the first empirical chapter, which focuses on the 1975 referendum campaign.

NOTES

1. These references are all taken from the Introduction section of the British National Party website http://www.bnp.org.uk/introduction (accessed on 15 November 2013).
2. Hansen (2006:51–4) describes this analytical technique as identifying basic discourses.

REFERENCES

Ashley, R. (1989). Living on border lines: Man, poststructuralism and war. In M. J. Shapiro & J. Der Derian (Eds.), *International/intertextual relations: Postmodern readings of world politics* (p. 353). Lexington, MA: Lexington.

Baker, D., & Schnapper, P. (2015). *Britain and the crisis of the European Union.* Basingstoke: Palgrave Macmillan.

Bakhtin, M. M., Holquist, M., & Emerson, C. (1981). *The dialogic imagination: Four essays.* University of Texas Press Slavic series. Austin: University of Texas Press. xxxiii, 443 p. pp.

Bartelson, J. (1995). *A genealogy of sovereignty.* Cambridge studies in international relations. Cambridge: Cambridge University Press. x, 317 p. pp.

Bevir, M., & Daddow, O. (2015). Interpreting foreign policy: National, comparative and regional studies. *International Relations, 29*(3), 273–287.

Bevir, M., Daddow, O., & Schnapper, P. (2015). Introduction: Interpreting British European policy. *JCMS: Journal of Common Market Studies, 53*(1), 1–17.

Booker, C., & North, R. (2005). *The great deception: Can the European Union survive?* (2nd ed). London: Continuum. xii, 643 p. pp.

Braun, M. (2008). Talking Europe—The dilemma of sovereignty and modernization. *Cooperation and Conflict, 43*(4), 397–420.

Buzan, B., Wæver, O., & de Wilde, J. (1998). *Security: A new framework for analysis.* Boulder, CO: Lynne Rienner. viii, 239 p. pp.

Campbell, D. (1998). *Writing security: United States foreign policy and the politics of identity* (Rev. ed.). Minneapolis: University of Minnesota Press. xiii, 289 p. pp.

Clough, P., & Nutbrown, C. (2002). *A student's guide to methodology: Justifying enquiry.* London: SAGE. xii, 212 p. pp.

Connolly, W. (1989). Identity and difference in World politics. In M. J. Shapiro & J. Der Derian (Eds.), *International/intertextual relations: Postmodern readings of world politics* (p. 353). Lexington, MA: Lexington.

Daddow, O. (2011). *New labour and the European Union: Blair and Brown's logic of history.* Machester: Manchester University Press.

de Wilde, P., & Trenz, H. J. (2012). Denouncing European integration: Euroscepticism as polity contestation. *European Journal of Social Theory, 15*(4), 537–554.

Der Derian, J. (1989). The boundaries of knowledge and power in international relations. In M. J. Shapiro & J. Der Derian (Eds.), *International/intertextual relations: Postmodern readings of world politics* (p. 353). Lexington, MA: Lexington.

Diez, T. (1997). Book Review: Henrik Larsen, Foreign Policy and Discourse Analysis: France, Britain and Europe (London: Routledge, 1997, 243 pp., £ 50.00 hbk.). *Millennium-Journal of International Studies, 26*(3): 931–933.

Diez, T. (2001). Europe as a discursive battleground: Discourse analysis and European integration studies. *Cooperation and Conflict, 36*(1), 5–38.

Diez, T. (2014). Setting the limits: Discourse and EU foreign policy. *Cooperation and Conflict, 49*(3), 319–333.

Dunn, K. C. (2008). Historical representations. In A. Klotz & D. Prakash (Eds.), *Qualitative methods in international relations: A pluralist guide* (pp. xii, 260 p.). Basingstoke: Palgrave Macmillan.

Emerson, M., Lannoo, K., Avery, G., Behrens, A., Ferrer, J. N., Beblavy, M., et al. (2015). *Britain's future in Europe: Reform, renegotiation, repatriation or secession?* Lanham, MD: Rowman & Littlefield International.

Fearon, J. D., & Laitin, D. D. (2000). Violence and the social construction of ethnic identity. *International Organization, 54*(4), 845–877.

Finnemore, M., & Sikkink, K. (1998). International norm dynamics and political change. *International Organization, 52*(4), 887–917.

Ford, R., Goodwin, M. J., & Cutts, D. (2012). Strategic Eurosceptics and polite xenophobes: Support for the United Kingdom Independence Party (UKIP) in the 2009 European Parliament elections. *European Journal of Political Research, 51*(2), 204–234.

Foucault, M., & Gordon, C. (1980). *Power/knowledge: Selected interviews and other writings, 1972–1977.* Brighton: Harvester. xi, 270 p. pp.

Fournier, P. (2012). Michel Foucault's considerable sway on international relations theory. *Bridges: Conversations in Global Politics and Public Policy, 1*(1), 18–43.

Gaskarth, J. (2006). Discourses and ethics: The social construction of British foreign policy. *Foreign Policy Analysis, 2*(4), 325–341.

Gee, J. P. (2011). *An introduction to discourse analysis: Theory and method* (3rd ed.). New York: Routledge. 218 p. pp.

Gibbins, J. (2014). *Britain, Europe and national identity: Self and other in international relations.* Basingstoke: Palgrave Macmillan.

Gifford, C. (2014a). *The making of Eurosceptic Britain.* Farnham: Ashgate Publishing.

Gifford, C. (2014b). The people against Europe: The Eurosceptic challenge to the United Kingdom's coalition government. *JCMS: Journal of Common Market Studies, 52*(3), 512–528.

Græger, N. (2005). Norway between NATO, the EU, and the US: A case study of post-cold war security and defence discourse. *Cambridge Review of International Affairs, 18*(1), 85–103.

Hansen, L. (2006). *Security as practice: Discourse analysis and the Bosnian war*. London: Routledge. xxiii, 259 p. pp.

Hansen, L. (2007). *The clash of cartoons? The clash of civilizations? Media and identity in the Danish 2006 cartoon case*. International Studies Association 48th Annual Convention, Hilton Chicago, Chicago, IL.

Hofferberth, M., & Weber, C. (2015). Lost in translation: A critique of constructivist norm research. *Journal of International Relations and Development, 18*(1), 75–103.

Huysmans, J. (2006). *The politics of insecurity: Fear, migration, and asylum in the EU*. The new international relations. Oxon: Routledge.

Jørgensen, M., Phillips, L., & Sage Publications. (2002). *Discourse analysis as theory and method*. London: SAGE.

Kenny, M. (2015). The return of 'Englishness' in British political culture—The end of the unions? *JCMS: Journal of Common Market Studies, 53*(1), 35–51.

Keohane, R. O. (1988). International institutions—2 approaches. *International Studies Quarterly, 32*(4), 379–396.

Kopecký, P., & Mudde, C. (2002). The two sides of euroscepticism party positions on european integration in east central europe. *European Union Politics, 3*(3), 297–326.

Larsen, H. (1997). *Foreign policy and discourse analysis: France, Britain, and Europe*. Routledge advances in international relations and politics. London: Routledge/LSE. vi, 243 p. pp.

Larsen, H. (1999). British and Danish European policies in the 1990s: A discourse approach. *European Journal of International Relations, 5*(4), 451–483.

Liddle, R. (2014). *The Europe dilemma: Britain and the drama of EU Integration*. London: IB Tauris.

Ludlow, N. P. (2015). Safeguarding british identity or betraying it? The role of British 'tradition'in the parliamentary great debate on EC membership, October 1971. *JCMS: Journal of Common Market Studies, 53*(1), 18–34.

Medrano, J. D. (2003). *Framing Europe: Attitudes to European integration in Germany, Spain, and the United Kingdom*. Princeton, NJ: Princeton University Press.

Neumann, I. B. (1999). *Uses of the other: "The East" in European identity formation*. Manchester: Manchester University Press. xv, 281 p. pp.

Neumann, I. B. (2008). Discourse analysis. In A. Klotz & D. Prakash (Eds.), *Qualitative methods in international relations: A pluralist guide* (pp. xii, 260 p.). Basingstoke: Palgrave Macmillan.

Rabinow, P. (1991). *The foucault reader.* London: Penguin.

Seldon, A., & Snowdon, P. (2015). *Cameron at 10: The inside story 2010–2015* (Kindle ed.). London: HarperCollins Publishers.

Shapiro, M. J. (1989). Textualising global politics. In M. J. Shapiro & J. Der Derian (Eds.), *International/intertextual relations: Postmodern readings of World politics* (353 p.). Lexington, MA: Lexington.

Spiering, M. (2014). *A cultural history of British Euroscepticism.* Basingstoke: Palgrave Macmillan.

Taggart, P. A., & Szczerbiak, A. (2001). *Parties, positions and Europe: Euroscepticism in the EU candidate states of Central and Eastern Europe.* Brighton: Sussex European Institute. 38 p. pp.

Taggart, P. A., & Szczerbiak, A. (2002). *The party politics of Euroscepticism in EU member and candidate states.* Brighton: Sussex European Institute.

Tajfel, H., & Turner, J. (1986). The social identity theory of intergroup behavior. In S. Worchel & W.G. Austin (Eds.), *The Psychology of Intergroup Relations* (pp. 7–24). Chicago: Nelson-Hall.

Tournier-Sol, K., & Gifford, C. (2015). *The UK challenge to Europeanization: The persistence of British Euroscepticism* (Kindle ed.). Basingstoke: Palgrave Macmillan.

Vasilopoulou, S. (2013). Continuity and change in the study of Euroscepticism: Plus ça change? *JCMS: Journal of Common Market Studies, 51*(1), 153–168.

Wæver, O. (2002). Identity, communities and foreign policy: Discourse analysis as foreign policy. In L. Hansen & O. Wæver (Eds.), *European integration and national identity: The challenge of the Nordic states,* pp. xii, 232 p. London: Routledge.

Walker, R. B. J. (1989). 'The Prince' and the pauper: Tradition, modernity and practice in the Theory of International Relations. In M. J. Shapiro & J. Der Derian (Eds.), *International/intertextual relations: Postmodern readings of World politics* (p. 353 p.). Lexington, MA: Lexington.

Walker, R. B. J. (1995). History and structure in the theory of international relations. In J. Der Derian (Ed.), *International theory: Critical investigations.* Basingstoke: Macmillan. pp. xxii, 407 p.

Wendt, A. (1995). Constructing international politics. *International Security, 20*(1), 71–81.

Wight, M. (1995). Why is there no international theory? In J. Der Derian (Ed.), *International theory: Critical investigations* (pp. xxii, 407 p.). Basingstoke: Macmillan.

Young, H. (1998). *This blessed plot: Britain and Europe from Churchill to Blair.* London: Macmillan. xiv, 558, 24 p. of plates pp.

CHAPTER 3

The British Discourse on Europe 1975: Wilson and the First Referendum

Abstract This chapter focuses on the period of the 1975 referendum, providing the basis on which to analyse the changes and continuities in the discourse. This period is of particular interest given Harold Wilson's gambit of renegotiation then referendum has since been echoed by David Cameron. The chapter gives a useful indication of how the issues were debated during the first referendum, identifying three major themes in the discourse as *Economy, Jobs and Trade*; *Agriculture, Food, and Fisheries*; and *Sovereignty and Democracy*. The anti-Marketeer (i.e. anti-EEC) representations of grave loss of sovereignty and coercion via secret deals in Brussels are employed in similar ways by Eurosceptics today.

Keywords Referendum • Sovereignty • Democracy • Economy • Agriculture and food prices

The UK joined the EEC in 1973 on the basis of a Parliamentary vote; once the European Communities Act 1972 had been passed by both the House of Commons and the House of Lords, the way was clear for accession to the EEC. Accession was negotiated and delivered under Ted Heath's Conservative government and was disputed by the then Labour opposition under the leadership of Harold Wilson.

The year after accession there were two general elections, the first producing a hung Parliament and the second a Labour majority. This meant Harold Wilson became Prime Minister for the second time. His job was

© The Editor(s) (if applicable) and The Author(s) 2016
J. Todd, *The UK's Relationship with Europe*,
DOI 10.1007/978-3-319-33669-5_3

to keep together a party divided by Europe whilst dealing with a range of deeply challenging economic issues; this may be ringing bells for observers of David Cameron's predicament over recent times. Having opposed accession to the EEC in 1973, Wilson had to come up with a plausible approach to managing the tricky issue of Europe. This he did via a commitment to renegotiate the UK's terms of membership and a commitment to a referendum following this renegotiation (this too should sound familiar for observers of modern British politics). This chapter focuses, therefore, on the period of the 1975 referendum, which asked the people of the United Kingdom the following question: *Do you think the UK should stay in the European Community (Common Market)?*

Over this period, the Conservative Party was relatively united in favour of EEC membership, whilst Labour was deeply divided. Those on the left of the Labour Party were most strongly against the EEC ("anti-Marketeers'" in the parlance of the day), whilst the more centrist party members were "pro-Marketeers." As a result of Labour divisions, the debates on membership involved the highly unusual step of suspending collective responsibility in the Cabinet. Normally, those who fundamentally disagree with the Government must resign from Ministerial office. However, Wilson decided that it was necessary to suspend this convention in order to prevent his party from imploding (David Cameron has since followed suit regarding the forthcoming referendum campaign). Indeed, some argue that the whole process of renegotiation and referendum was more about internal party management than the high politics of EEC membership. For example, Young mentions an interview with former Foreign Office official Michael Butler, in which Butler recounts a meeting with the then Foreign Secretary Jim Callaghan. When asked by Callaghan if he "really cared" about Europe, Butler replied in the affirmative. The Foreign Secretary accepted this stance with a fairly hefty caveat: "Very well. But just remember, I really care about the Labour Party" (quoted in Young 1998:279). Similarly, Booker and North refer to Harold Wilson's senior policy advisor at the time, Brian Donoghue, describing his claim that renegotiation "was a stratagem to suppress internal party dissent" (Booker and North 2005:202–3). This theme also features in the following analysis.

The referendum campaign was led for the "Yes" campaign by Roy Jenkins, whilst the "No" campaign's two highest profile members were the archetypal political odd couple Tony Benn and Enoch Powell. The leaders of both main parties eschewed a prominent role in the campaign; both

Wilson and the newly appointed leader of the Conservatives, Margaret Thatcher, provided relatively low-key support to the "Yes" campaign. The referendum took place on 5 June 1975, with 67.2% voting "Yes" and 32.8% voting "No."

The aforementioned grievous economic conditions need to be set out in slightly more detail. The first election of 1974 was precipitated by the infamous "three-day week," when a dispute with the miners brought both the economy and Heath's Conservative government to their knees. As Young describes it, "the country saw itself being in desperate economic straits" as a result of "the economic damage and national trauma" of the three-day week (Young 1998:288–9). In addition, the UK had to cope with what Booker and North (2005:202) describe as "Soaring wage demands and the quadrupling of world oil prices [that] led to galloping inflation." Another brief bit of context to include is the status of the European Free Trade Association (EFTA). EFTA was originally conceived by the UK as an alternative to the Treaty of Rome to include "all of the trade and none of the politics" (Young 1998:115). The other founding members were Denmark, Sweden, Norway, Austria, Portugal, and Switzerland, though by 1975 Denmark had also joined the EEC. Currently, EFTA is made up of four countries (Iceland, Liechtenstein, Norway, and Switzerland), and is held up by some Eurosceptics as an alternative to UK membership of the EU (see van Randwyck 2011).

Regarding the research questions, this chapter provides the basis on which to analyse the *changes* and *continuities* in the discourse. The chapter will give a useful indication of how the issues were debated during the first referendum; whilst the issues themselves might change—and the context certainly will—the tone and descriptive content might well stay the same. The discourse analysed in this chapter is drawn from the following sources:

- The campaign literature for the referendum. There were three key pieces of literature that were sent to every household in the country: a booklet from Britain in Europe (the "Yes" campaign), a booklet from the National Referendum Campaign (the somewhat uninspiring name for the "No" campaign), and a booklet from the Government (which also recommended a "yes" vote). The two-to-one ratio of "yes" to "no" booklets matches almost perfectly with the referendum result.
- The Parliamentary debate on the *White Paper on the Membership of the European Community*. In the words of Prime Minister Harold

Wilson, the debate was where the House of Commons was "called upon to assess the outcome of the renegotiations of the terms of British entry into the European Community and the wider issues involved in the decision whether to remain in the Community or to leave it" (Hansard 1974–1975:889 col. 821).[1] The debate took place over three days (7–9 April 1975), with the speeches totalling over 150,000 words of discourse.[2]

• Newspaper editorials from 1975 that mention the referendum. The editorials were drawn from *The Times*, the *Daily Express,* and the *Daily Mirror* (40 articles in all).

Overall, there were two positions present in the discourse (this is unsurprising given the yes/no nature of the referendum campaign). The campaign literature proved particularly helpful in identifying key themes debated by those occupying the two positions. All three booklets— "Yes," "No," and Government—contain sections on jobs/trade, food prices, and Britain's democratic traditions. The Parliamentary debates and editorials aligned with the campaign literature. I also note that Larsen (1999:460) has previously observed that "'parliamentary sovereignty' is a pivot or nodal point in the British discourse on the state/nation, and central in relation to Europe." I, therefore, determined there to be three major themes and one minor theme present. I term the three major themes as *Economy, Jobs and Trade; Agriculture, Food, and Fisheries;* and *Sovereignty and Democracy.* The minor theme I label as *Consequences for Peace and Security.* I also include a brief section on *Portrayals of Party Division* before the chapter Conclusion. This analyses how the party divisions which permeate the discourse are framed by both the media and other political actors.

Linkages exist between the issues. For example, importing food clearly links economy, jobs, and trade with agriculture, food, and fisheries. There are a number of subtexts that run through the discourse related to colonial guilt (though some exhibit more of a wistful longing for days of Empire), the impact of the world wars, and a general sense of insecurity and concern about the UK's place in the world. Other points of interest from a modern perspective include arguments that "cherry-picking" favourable parts of the European deal would be unrealistic, and arguments about the permanent and binding nature of the Treaty of Accession.

Before moving to the first major theme, I note that each Parliamentary contributor whose part allegiance is not obvious (e.g. Wilson, Thatcher) has an abbreviated label after their name. These are L—Labour, C—Conservative, Lib—Liberal, SNP—Scottish National Party, and PC—Plaid Cymru. Where appropriate, I group quotes from similar sources (e.g. Labour pro-Marketeers).

3.1 ECONOMY, JOBS, AND TRADE

One major theme in the discourse, addressed by both pro- and anti-Marketeers in significant detail, is concerned with the implications of EEC membership for the economy, job market, and international trade (see Fig. 3.1). Given the EEC, by its very nature, was concerned with trade and economic matters, the presence of this theme is hardly surprising. The key representation of the pro-Marketeers against leaving was "why risk it?" Given the fragile nature of the UK economy at the time, this was an effective strategy. The anti-Marketeers also use the fragile economy to bolster their arguments, though they consider the EEC to be to blame. The following analysis begins with the debate on trade figures before moving to the prospects of EFTA membership. Finally, some high-level arguments regarding the effects of EEC membership on the British economy are featured.

As is often the case with figures relating to trade and economy, politicians and the media present such statistics in a variety of different ways, depending on their perspective. As Winifred Ewing (SNP) quips during the White Paper debate, "These are the conclusions on which I base my facts" (Hansard 1974–1975:889, col. 1111). For example, one anti-Marketeer (Roy Hughes, L) asserted that "The figures for January and February of this year given by the Secretary of State for Trade show that we now have a non-oil deficit with the other Common Market countries

Staying in protects our jobs

Jobs depend upon our industries investing more and being able to sell in the world. If we came out, our industry would be based on the smallest home market of any major exporting country in the world, instead of on the Community market of 250 million people.

Fig.3.1 Excerpt from "Yes" campaign booklet

running at an annual rate of £260 million. Our whole trade pattern has been distorted" (ibid.:893). Similarly, another (Teddy Taylor, C) claims that "With Europe we have moved from a non-oil credit of £132 million in 1970 to a non-oil deficit of £1800 million in 1974—a catastrophic reversal of the situation. This is a fact; it is not an assessment" (ibid.:896).

This theme is also picked up in the "No" campaign booklet in the section entitled "Huge trade deficit with Common Market" (Fig. 3.2). As can be observed in Fig. 3.2, the section argues that "The Common Market pattern of trade was never designed to suit Britain. According to our Department of Trade, our trade deficit with the Common Market was running, in the early months of 1975, at nearly £2600 million a year— a staggering figure, compared with a very small deficit in 1970 when we were free to trade in accordance with our own policies" (National Referendum Campaign 1975). The key representation here is the EEC as trade distorting.

The theme of trade is generally argued at a different level by the pro-Marketeers, with fewer detailed figures. Margaret Thatcher, for example, argues that "on the broad strategic trade and aid argument we have preferential access to Western Europe, with which we conduct 50 per cent of our trade. I doubt very much whether we should be able to get that on our own" (Hansard 1974–1975:889, col. 1025). Reginald Maudling

Huge trade deficit with Common Market

The Common Market pattern of trade was never designed to suit Britain.

According to our Department of Trade, our trade deficit with the Common Market was running, in the early months of 1975, at nearly £2,600 million a year–a staggering figure, compared with a very small deficit in 1970 when we were free to trade in accordance with our own policies.

Fig. 3.2   Excerpt from "No" campaign booklet

(C) argues strongly that "The grave trade deficit with the Community ... does not mirror the effect of membership of the Community. It mirrors our own failure as a nation to export, and it mirrors world conditions" (ibid.:1348). This theme is also addressed by another pro-Marketeer (Russell Johnston, Lib):

> [O]ur present relative failure as a country has come about outside the Community ... To attribute our low growth rate and our comparatively falling standard of living to entry into the Community in 1973, as many hon. Members have done, is grossly unfair. (ibid.:1334)

When analysing the two sides of the aforementioned debate, it is clear that negativity is a common theme. The anti-Marketeers frame the situation being "catastrophic," the trade deficit with the EEC "staggering," and that "Our whole trade pattern has been distorted." The pro-Marketeers acknowledge the deficit as "grave," the country's growth rate as low, and the standard of living as falling. However, the key discursive struggle is on where the blame for this situation lies. Placing the blame on EEC membership is an effective move for the anti-Marketeers, and their forceful use of Government statistics enables such bold claims as "This is a fact; it is not an assessment." These differing interpretations align with Shapiro's (1989:13) claim that "representations are not descriptions of a world of facticity, but are ways of making facticity"; the excerpt in the previous sentence is an example of this being explicitly attempted.

The prospect of EFTA as an alternative to EEC membership is addressed at some length in the Parliamentary debate and in the campaign literature. The "No" campaign argued that the EFTA countries "are now to enjoy free entry for their industrial exports into the Common Market without having to carry the burden of the Market's dear food policy or suffer rule from Brussels" (National Referendum Campaign 1975). The booklet goes on to assert that:

> Britain already enjoys industrial free trade with these countries. If we withdrew from the Common Market we should remain members of the wider group and enjoy, as the EFTA countries do, free or low-tariff entry into the Common Market countries without the burden of dear food or the loss of the British people's democratic rights. (ibid.)

This quote links explicitly to the other two major themes in the discourse through reference to food prices and loss of democracy. The "Yes" campaign, in contrast, states that "Some want us to be half linked to Europe, as part of a free trade area—but the European Community itself doesn't want that" (Britain in Europe Campaign 1975). An editorial in *The Times* from 31 May goes into significant detail on issues of trade and influence. The editorial argues that:

> whether in or out, Britain will be heavily dependent on trade with Europe; whether in or out, the conditions on which that trade will be done will be established by the European Community, primarily with a view to the national interest of the countries who comprise the Community. If in, we shall continue to play a full part in deciding what Community policy is. If out, we shall be almost, though not quite, as much affected by Community policy, but will have no hand in determining its course. (The Times 1975c)

Prime Minister Wilson, Margaret Thatcher, Geoffrey Howe (C), and Edward Heath (C) each continue this theme. All are major political figures who had a fundamental impact on the UK's relationship with Europe. They speak in favour of EEC membership, and the consistency of their message on the downsides of EFTA membership or a similar free trade agreement is noteworthy. The Prime Minister states that:

> Our friends, our former EFTA partners who have remained outside the Community but in association with it, have found that the EFTA-EEC agreements have required their assent, as a condition of those EFTA-EEC agreements, to precisely similar requirements, as a condition of trade agreements, as are in force within the Community itself, namely, and principally, measures to prevent the frustration of international competition by regional subsidies or other means. And of course it is self-evident that while Britain, within the Community, has the ability to negotiate changes in these requirements—and we have negotiated derogations from them so far as we are concerned—the EFTA countries have no part, no locus, in such negotiations. (Hansard 1974–1975:889, col. 830–831)

Margaret Thatcher supports this, affirming that "even if we could get into EFTA, that would be no answer to our problems" (ibid.:1031). Geoffrey Howe too states that "We should be faced with all the constraints of commercial and industrial policies and none of the advantages" (ibid.:1036). Finally, Edward Heath notes that "we would have no say in what was done by the Community. That would be a real and pointless sacrifice of sovereignty" (ibid.:1283). The point about lack of influence as a member of EFTA still resonates, with the current Norwegian experience being caricatured as "fax democracy" or "fax machine diplomacy" (see Ekman 2005; The Economist 2004). Edward Heath highlights the link here to issues of sovereignty and democracy. Other pro-Marketeers also make the link between economic well-being and sovereignty, with John Mackintosh (L) arguing that a "no" vote would also have sovereignty implications because of the potential that "We would have to go to the IMF for a loan, and then our sovereignty would be at stake" (Hansard 1974–1975:889, col. 878). William Hamilton (L) asserts that "The Chancellor is not exaggerating when he says that if we get out and the Arabs, as a consequence, withdraw all their money from the banks of this country we could be bankrupt in 48 hours" (ibid.:1342). This somewhat doom-laden theme is reinforced by Brian Walden (L), who warns that leaving the EEC "might give our fragile economy that final push over the precipice" (ibid.:1040). These pro-Marketeers represent the prospect of leaving as a threat to the UK's economy and, by extension, sovereignty.

This theme does not contain a significant degree of explicit identity politics. One can speculate that the UK's parlous economic position in 1975 made it difficult for either side to build a positive sense of identity at either a national or European level. In addition, any attempts at negative differentiation in such circumstances would have put the UK on the wrong side of the equation: unhelpful for either campaign.

In summarising this theme, I note that the tone of the debate was overwhelmingly negative. The two key representations of the economic implications of the referendum are the "why risk leaving?" representation employed by the pro-Marketeers and the "EEC as trade distorting" representation employed by the anti-Marketeers. Essentially, there is a discursive struggle to frame the UK's EEC membership as either a cause of the country's economic woes or part of the solution, with neither position dominant. This is interesting from a power-knowledge perspective, in that there appears to be a good degree of consensus about the economic mess the UK was in. However, there is a battle over the facticity of the causes of and solutions to this mess.

3.2   Agriculture, Food, and Fisheries

This theme encompasses debate about the effects of the Common Agricultural Policy (CAP) on the UK, in particular, with regard to food prices, and debate about whether or not Wilson's renegotiation achieved anything of substance with regard to agriculture and fisheries. Overall, the key representations on the anti-Marketeer side were of a rigid CAP and dearer food, whilst the pro-Marketeers side represented EEC membership as providing security of food supply (see Fig. 3.3). The section begins with the 1975 renegotiation; this is of interest given the more recent attempts at renegotiation by the UK Government.

The White Paper debate on the renegotiation of the CAP gets off to an inauspicious start, with the Prime Minister acknowledging that, in regard to his renegotiation commitment, "we have not secured the objectives we there set out—I am being perfectly fair about this—for example in the fundamental alterations we called for in CAP" (Hansard 1974–1975:889, col.822). Others in favour of EEC membership sought to make the best of the renegotiations. The Minister for Agriculture, Food, and Fisheries argues that "the changes we have secured in the beef régime are evidence of a welcome flexibility in the operation of the CAP. We attach great importance to this last point so as to enable special circumstances to be dealt with in different parts of the Community" (ibid.:1249). The Government's referendum booklet claims that "as a result of these negotiations, the Common Market's agricultural policy (known as CAP) now works more flexibly to the benefit of both housewives[3] and farmers" (HM Government 1975:8). Nonetheless, the general consensus even among pro-Marketeers aligned with the point made by Kenneth Lomas (L) that "As for the common agricultural policy, of course much remains to be done" (Hansard 1974–1975:889, col.904). *The Times* addresses the issue of agriculture and CAP reform several times in 1975. Before the referendum, the newspaper notes that "The issue which once seemed the main stumbling-block of British membership, the Common Agricultural Policy, has now been virtually shelved, mainly because that policy now appears

Secure food at fair prices

Before we joined the Community everyone feared that membership would mean paying more for our food than if we were outside. This fear has proved wrong. **If anything, the Community has saved us money on food in the past two years.**

Fig. 3.3   Excerpt from the "Yes" campaign booklet

much less disadvantageous for Britain than it did two years ago" (The Times 1975d). Later in 1975, the newspaper calls for CAP reform, urging that "Both Britain and West Germany should use this year's budget exercise to press for some real results from the endless and so far fruitless stock-taking of the CAP" (The Times 1975b).

The anti-Marketeers were, of course, strident in their criticism of the renegotiation during the White Paper debate, with Teddy Taylor (C) arguing that "Despite the assurance that a major change in the CAP would be vital if Britain were to remain in the Common Market, we have had no change whatsoever" (Hansard 1974–1975:889, col. 898). Another anti-Marketeer (D.E. Thomas, PC) asserts that "there has been no fundamental renegotiation of the common agricultural policy" (ibid.:863). Donald Stewart (SNP), representing the Western Isles of Scotland, picked up on Harold Wilson's acknowledgement regarding the CAP negotiations. He states that "The right hon. Gentleman the Prime Minister admitted in his speech this afternoon that the renegotiations had not changed the fundamental character of the common agricultural policy. Speaking as a Scot, I regard that as a disaster—although I am aware that England also has its agricultural industry" (ibid.:884). Naturally, no debate about agriculture would be complete without reference to the French (by Frank Hooley, L): "Let nobody suppose that the French Government would for one moment remain within the Common Market if anyone threatened the CAP" (ibid.:1048). Enoch Powell (C) is clear in his view that the renegotiations achieved "not a single alteration whatsoever in the terms of British membership of the Community" (ibid.:1298). We can observe some elements of nationalism in the discourse here, both on behalf of the Scottish agricultural industry and through negative reference to French entrenchment regarding the CAP. Modern hard Eurosceptics are at least as forceful as their anti-Marketeer forebears in their criticism of the results of David Cameron's renegotiation.

The anti-Marketeers were also critical with regard to fisheries. One Scottish Nationalist Party MP (Winifred Ewing) takes up the cause of Scottish fishing: "Why was fishing omitted? Why was fishing not even on the agenda? ... A totally unified industry was there for the first time because it did not want the EEC fisheries policy to come into force on 1st January 1984" (ibid.:1111–2). Margaret Thatcher, despite her pro-Market stance, acknowledges that "I agree that fishing has not yet been fully resolved in the treaty" (ibid.:1031). It is noteworthy that the Minister for Agriculture, Food, and Fisheries singularly neglects to mention fishing in his speech; this is surely unusual given his policy responsibility for fisheries. The Prime Minister only mentions fishing following an intervention from the floor, and his response can at best be characterised as muddled (see column 835 of the debate). It appears that those on the pro-Market side were well aware that the renegotiations on fisheries had achieved little to nothing of substance and therefore sought to silence the issue.

The more general debate on the effects of the CAP and EEC membership on agriculture and food prices ranged from a narrow focus on food prices in the UK to broader points about living standards in the developing world. Anti-Marketeers sought to convince that food prices had increased as a consequence of membership. Norman Buchan (L) asserts "Let us hear no more rubbish about the EEC not pushing up food prices. It has done so dramatically, and will continue to do for the next year or two" (ibid.:1272). The following quote from Ernest Fernyhough (L) makes a point about denaturing of agricultural produce:

> On our television screens, week after week in the past few months, we have had pictures of starving people in Ethiopia, Bangladesh, Vietnam and other countries; and here we are saying that it is very desirable for us to tie ourselves, hook, line and sinker as it were, to a system which believes in building up big stocks of meat, butter, cheese and milk and destroying and denaturing wheat. How can we as a so-called civilised, Christian people ever defend the regulations and rules of a system which on the one hand puts into storage millions of tons of food and on the other does nothing at a time when stomachs are empty to marry that food to those empty stomachs? (ibid.:1075)

This quote is a hard-hitting combination of ethical and spatial dimensions of identity, with references to "we as a so-called civilised, Christian people" and "starving people in Ethiopia, Bangladesh, Vietnam and other countries." Fernyhough employs these dimensions to criticise the CAP as a system that "does nothing" to feed the needy with the stockpiles of produce built up under CAP "regulations and rules." It is also possible to observe here a claim that "the people" (either in other countries or the "civilised" British) are being made to suffer, either physically or in terms of their morals, at the hands of an uncaring "system."

Those in favour of EEC membership also combine pragmatic and principled arguments. On the pragmatic side, the pro-Marketeers make repeated reference to security and stability of food supplies. For example,

Roy Hattersley (L) propounds that "the conclusion must be that not only is stability and security for our supplies obtained by EEC membership but that over the past year we are not paying any more for our food than we would have paid had we not joined the Community" (ibid.:956). This point is echoed from across the floor of the debating chamber by Margaret Thatcher:

> We are the most vulnerable country with our need for food imports. Therefore, it is vital that we secure access to continuous and good sources of food supply. In some years supplies from the Continent will be more expensive; in other years they will be cheaper. But the great benefit is access and greater stability of supplies. (ibid.:1024)

Reginald Maudling (C) takes a different approach, stating to good effect that "We cannot go in and out of the Community like a yo-yo depending on the price of grain in the Chicago market" (ibid.:1347). The *Daily Mirror* employs what could be described as commercial intertextuality with regard to food prices. An editorial highlights the views of both Marks and Spencer and Sainsbury, noting that "Most housewives would reckon that these two firms know their way around when it comes to value and efficiency. And both firms think membership of the Common Market is good value for Britain" (Daily Mirror 1975b).

Overall, the tone of the debate under Agriculture, Food, and Fisheries appears less negative than that of Economy, Jobs, and Trade. However, there remain many negative points in the generally pragmatic debate on prices and security/stability of supply, with the discourse leavened occasionally by calls to principle, most often from a perspective of helping the disadvantaged abroad. The key contestation was between representations of the EEC and CAP as rigid and unchanged despite the renegotiations, and the EEC as providing stability and security of food supply.

3.3   SOVEREIGNTY AND DEMOCRACY

The debates on the implications of EEC membership for the UK's sovereignty and democracy form the third of the three major themes in 1975. The White Paper debates on these matters contained *relatively* little of the jingoism that one might expect, given the sensitivity of the topic and the more frenetic tone of contemporary debates (see Chap. 5). The debates are marked by a general (though not unanimous) acknowledgement that sovereignty had been lost/transferred as a consequence of EEC member-ship. The disagreements therefore tended to focus more on whether this was a positive development or not. The key anti-Marketeer representation here was of the EEC as anti-democratic, authoritarian, and a threat to sov-ereignty (see Fig. 3.4). Pro-Marketeers, meanwhile, represented the EU has enhancing de facto sovereignty.

This section begins by presenting the arguments presented by the anti-Marketeers. The "No" campaign booklet argues that the Common Market shall "merge Britain with France, Germany, Italy and other countries into a single nation. This will take away from us the right to rule ourselves which we have enjoyed for centuries" (National Referendum Campaign 1975). During the White Paper debate, Nigel Spearing (L) argued that "The Common Market executive in the Commission and in the Council is a supranational authority which is basically hierarchical in nature and in the end requires coercion rather than consent" (Hansard 1974–1975:889, col. 915). A similar point was made by Renee Short (L): "If we remain in the Common Market, this Parliament will no longer be the supreme law-making body, and we shall have to abide by the laws that are made by the Community for ever and a day, as long as we remain within the Common Market" (ibid.:934–5). Neil Marten (C) asserted that

> We have got ourselves into a position where, despite pre-discussion, laws are finalised by wheeling and dealing in secret in Brussels. … Ministers go[ing] back to Brussels on behalf of the British people, wheeling and deal-ing behind the scenes, and coming up with something entirely different from what was presented to this House. In that way this House has lost its sovereignty. (ibid.:1059)

These quotes contain some of the key tenets of modern Euroscepticism: fears of being subsumed into a European super-state, coercion and "wheel-

Fig. 3.4   Section header from "No" campaign booklet

ing and dealing in secret" in Brussels, and overall loss of sovereignty. It is fair to say that these concerns, whilst particularly acute in the British discourse, appear in many other European countries as well (see Harmsen and Spiering 2004). Temporal dimensions of identity are invoked to describe the UK as being at risk of losing the independence it has enjoyed "for centuries" and that the country might be forced to abide by EEC law "for ever and a day."

Other anti-Marketeers sought to ratchet up the debate, including Teddy Taylor (C): "we have a long-term historic tradition of democratic control and decision making, and although certain European countries follow the British pattern they do not have the long-term commitment to democratic control, nor is this seen in the institutions of Europe" (ibid.:903). Douglas Jay (L), one of the higher profile anti-Marketeers, has the following emotive contribution on the subject:

> We are left with an authoritarian system of legislation, taxation and government which is already sapping away not just the sovereignty of this country as an independent self-governing nation but the democratic control of our people over the laws and powers of government. To my mind, that is more important than what is normally called sovereignty...
>
> To accept this type of authoritarian rule is to go back on a democratic principle which has been taken for granted in this country for nearly three centuries; namely, that legislation must be approved by representatives of the people. The right hon. Member for Penrith and the Border (Mr. Whitelaw) spoke today about the two world wars in this century. Some of us who lived through those two wars—I had always supposed all of us—believed that we were fighting, amongst other things, for the preservation of government by the people for the people in these islands. (ibid.:860–1)

These quotations take a more overtly nationalist tone, with the UK linked to a "long-term historic tradition" of democracy and differentiated from a Continental other embodied by an "authoritarian system of legislation, taxation, and government" that was "sapping away" British sovereignty and democracy. It is noteworthy to see an anti-Marketeer using reference to the Second World War; this most violent and significant of conflicts is referenced by all sides of the debate through the years. The different interpretations of the lessons of the Second World War are illuminating. Those in favour of the European project speak about the horrors of the war to claim that a united Europe is necessary to avoid any repetition: this is the temporal othering described by Diez (2004).

Those against the project discuss the war in terms of having protected British sovereignty from the continent and that this protection should continue: in extreme cases some Eurosceptics have claimed the EU is akin to Nazi Germany (see, e.g. Heffer 2013). Returning to the aforementioned quotes, reference to "these islands" is a programmatic catchphrase. This catchphrase reinforces both the UK's separate identity—one has to only think of the famous (if most likely apocryphal) headline "Fog in the Channel, Continent cut off"—from the rest of Europe and the threat that the UK faced during the Second World War. The English Channel is thus implicitly invoked as both a physical and historical manifestation of Neumann and Ashley's slash between an island self/Continental other. Given the long history of threats of invasion across the Channel (from the Normans in 1066, through the Spanish Armada and Napoleonic France, to Nazi Germany), this is an effective way of framing the issue on behalf of the anti-Marketeers.

Enoch Powell also addresses the theme of nationalism in his speech, which focused entirely on the themes of sovereignty and democracy:

> [T]he hon. Member for Ladywood also accused me of being a nationalist. If by nationalist is meant that I believe that the habits, the genius, the character and the institutions of one country can be compared upon a sort of scale with those of other countries and that they can be assigned an order of merit on some such scale, in that sense I am not a nationalist and never have been. However, I am a nationalist in the sense that I believe that a nation has a certain genius or character of its own and that its institutions conform themselves to that character or genius. I believe that they cannot be denied or renounced without danger and destruction to that nation itself, and that they cannot, for the same reason, merely be transferred to others whose genius is different. I believe that the Government of this country under a Parliament which has the sole right to legislate and to tax, with an unwritten constitution which leaves the whole defence of the subject as well as the welfare of the country in the hands of this House, corresponds uniquely to the genius of its people. (ibid.:1303–4)

This is an interesting excerpt, with Powell appearing to dabble in constructivism. He affirms that each nation has a distinct identity ("genius or character of its own," in his words), and that this identity defines the nature of that nation's institutions. Powell goes on to argue that this defining link between identity and institutions means that damaging such institutions cannot be done without "danger and destruction to that nation itself." The final sentence of the quote is somewhat delphic in its structure, though it can be understood as Powell arguing that a sovereign and independent Parliament is the institution that "corresponds uniquely" with British national identity—that is, to the exclusion of any other institutions such as the EEC. Overall, Powell uses an argument about the mutually constitutive nature of national identity and national institutions to justify his strong opposition to EEC membership. There is a clear demarcation of a national self in danger from the European other. This demarcation is also observed by Marcussen et al. (1999:627), who state that "The collective identification with national symbols, history and institutions is far greater in the British political discourse than a potential identification with European symbols, history and institutions." Ludlow's analysis of the "Parliamentary Great Debate" on entry into the EEC observed that those opposed to membership also raised concerns about "the incompatibility between European supranationalism and British notions of parliamentary sovereignty" (2015:26): these concerns are clearly still present in 1975 (and indeed today).

The anti-Marketeers hold a stronger position in the discourse than the pro-Marketeers when it comes to the issue of sovereignty, though far from one of crushing dominance. The Government's referendum booklet argues that whilst EEC membership "imposes new rights and duties on Britain," it "does not deprive us of our national identity." (HM Government 1975:11). Roy Hattersley (L) makes a strong point on democracy and sovereignty:

> I do not believe that when the people of Great Britain discuss sovereignty they are thinking of the rights and responsibilities of the House of Commons, whose literal and material powers have diminished as Great Britain has moved from the role of a world Power to the position of a medium-sized Power. Sovereignty is the right or the ability of the British Government to take what decisions seem right to them on behalf of the British people. Those decisions, and the ability to take them, are much more conditioned by economic power and our political influence in the world than by the procedures of this House. (Hansard 1974–1975:889, col. 959)

Geoffrey Howe (C) too takes this perspective:

> I believe that continued membership will act to the benefit of true sovereignty, sovereignty of the kind for which we have striven as elected representatives—namely, our power to influence our own destiny and our power, as

elected representatives, to act on behalf of the people. That is what I mean by sovereignty. I believe that that will be enhanced rather than diminished by continued membership of the Community. (ibid.:1139)

These arguments are an interesting expansion of some of the points made about the UK's economic prospects being enhanced by EEC membership. However, the tone when speaking in more general terms about the UK's prospects is more optimistic than when speaking about economic matters. It is worth noting that the arguments in favour of UK membership continue to be framed in terms of what the EEC can do for the UK, rather than what the UK might do for the EEC. Also, the arguments relating to sovereignty and democracy from the pro-Marketeers are far from monolithic. For example, here are two Labour pro-Marketeers, Maurice Edelman and Evan Luard, with different takes on the issue:

Edelman: I believe that that willing surrender of sovereignty for a specific end, with delegation of power for a particular purpose, is wholly desirable. Those of us who support the idea of the European Economic Community should not feel any sense of shame or diffidence about affirming that we are in favour of this limited cession of sovereignty for a specific purpose. (ibid.:1103–4)

Luard: To my mind it is a fact that entry into the Community involves this country in some loss of sovereignty. This is one of the prime reasons why we should wish to join in that endeavour … I suppose that for those of us who regard ourselves as internationalists, for those of us who want above everything else the monopoly of power at present centred in the nation State to be merged in wider associations of States, for those of us who believe that the prime task for national governments in the modern age is to join their neighbours in joint arrangements, there is still a reason for supporting regional organisations as well as international institutions. (ibid.:1318–9)

Luard's view is unsurprising given his later academic works, which address the idea of an international society and drew praise from Hedley Bull (see Roberts 1992:71). Edelman takes a narrower and more pragmatic view, arguing that any loss of sovereignty is justifiable for "a specific purpose." So, once again, we can observe both pragmatic and principled arguments in favour of EEC membership. The arguments about sovereignty and democracy are addressed at length in an editorial in *The Times* from 31 April. The editorial notes that the two sides are addressing different conceptualisations of sovereignty, judging that the pro-Marketeers "equate sovereignty with power," whilst the anti-Marketeers define it as "a juridical concept" (The Times 1975e). The editorial concludes that:

> The extent to which each person shares the fears or hopes which surround the two formulations will depend partly on how he understands the dynamics of contemporary political society and partly on how he sees the European Community developing. (ibid.)

The issue of how EEC membership affected the judicial system was relatively underplayed when compared to discussion of its effect on Parliament. Enoch Powell argues that "membership of the European Community requires from this House and this country a renunciation of Parliament's sole right to authorise the laws and taxes of this country and requires from this country a renunciation of the right to be judged in the courts of this land" (Hansard 1974–1975:889, col. 1296). Renee Short (L) employs explicit intertextuality in quoting Lord Justice Denning's famous phrase[4] that, in its effect on the courts system, "the Treaty of Rome is like an oncoming tide. It flows into the estuaries and up the rivers—it cannot be held back" (ibid.:935). On the pro-Market side, Reginald Maudling (C) was more relaxed:

> Of course it is true that the treaty involves the acceptance and enforcement by the British courts of Community law. But there are many examples of treaties which oblige us to enact legislation which is effective in the British courts. I cannot see very great differences in practice between being obliged ourselves to enact the legislation or telling the courts to follow legislation which has been enacted by a body of which we are a member. (ibid.:1351–2)

The 'Yes' campaign booklet claims that "Common law is not affected. For a few commercial and industrial purposes there is need for Community Law. But our criminal law, trial by jury, presumption of innocence remain unaltered" (Britain in Europe Campaign 1975). Turning to the media, *The Times* notes that:

> We now have a source of law external to the state, and also external to the state a court, the European Court, supervisory and activist in the continental tradition, empowered ultimately to interpret and implement the Treaties

and their consequential provisions. This is indeed the matter of sovereignty. (The Times 1975a)

There is differentiation here via reference to a "continental tradition" of jurisprudence that is "supervisory and activist."

The debates about sovereignty and democracy in 1975 have, perhaps, more resonance for modern observers than the previous two themes. The anti-Marketeer arguments about grave loss of sovereignty and coercion via secret deals in Brussels are employed in similar ways by Eurosceptics currently. It is also possible to observe differentiation between self and other, with a sovereign British self at threat from a Continental other that lacks a strong commitment to democratic ideals. In the Parliamentary debates, the anti-Marketeer representation of the EEC as anti-democratic, authoritarian, and a threat to sovereignty is somewhat stronger than the main pro-Marketeer representation of the EEC as enhancing British sovereignty.

3.4   Consequences for Peace and Security

One more minor theme present in the discourse is the consequences of EEC membership for peace and security. This is dominated by the pro-Marketeers and their fears for European security in the event of the UK leaving the EEC. The "Yes" campaign booklet asserts that EEC membership "makes good sense for world peace" (Britain in Europe Campaign 1975). Margaret Thatcher states that "One of the measures of the success of the Community that we now take for granted is essentially security. I think that security is a matter not only of defence but of working together in peacetime on economic issues which concern us and of working closely together on trade, work and other social matters which affect all our peoples" (Hansard 1974–1975 889 col. 1023). Edward Heath warns that "I do not believe that NATO can carry out its proper purpose effectively if Europe shows signs of disintegrating and fragmenting within the Community" (ibid.: 1280). The following quotes from George Sinclair (C), Tom Arnold (C), and Maurice Edelman (L) build on this theme, warning of negative implications of a divided Europe. Sinclair argues that:

> The main identity of interest [shared across Europe] is political. It is in security and defence for the people of the West working in unity. If that is not achieved, we shall face two threats: first, that Europe will again be divided

and will tear itself apart, and, secondly, that we shall not be strong enough to stand against the military strength of the USSR. (ibid.:1092)

Arnold asserts that "The circumstances of our post-war world, if we are to avoid a future holocaust, dictate that those interests require a compromise with the nations of Europe, expressed through the European Community" (ibid.:1325). Finally, Edelman argues against nationalism, using name checking as a form of authority-building intertextuality:

> What we wanted to do at this first great meeting of the Council of Europe, which was attended by Hugh Dalton, Herbert Morrison and Winston Churchill, was to seek the economic and political integration of Europe and to put an end to the Balkanisation of Europe, which was the origin of the fratricidal wars which had continued for over a century. Our purpose was to try to avoid the tribal nationalisms which in the past have bedevilled, and even today still bedevil, the condition of Europe. (ibid.:1101)

These quotes highlight two "others" as threats to European peace and security. One, straightforwardly enough given the ongoing Cold War, is the USSR. The second is described by Diez in his article *Europe's Others and the Return of Geopolitics* as follows: "the most important other in the construction of a European identity has been Europe's own past" (Diez 2004:319). The three quotes refer to previous "fratricidal wars," the "Balkanisation of Europe," threats of "a future holocaust," or that Europe once again "will tear itself apart." Diez describes this as "temporal othering" (ibid.:321), and it aligns with Hansen's description of using temporal dimensions of identity to differentiate between self and other. With regard to the self, Sinclair explicitly refers to Europe having a "main identity of interest" based on security and defence. Pro-Marketeers use the self/other approach in their attempts to define a shared European sense of self as part of their justification for the UK's continued membership of the EEC.

3.5   PORTRAYALS OF PARTY DIVISION

The division of the two main political parties over Europe permeates the discourse. The divisions help demonstrate the importance of the European issue in British politics. Given the aforementioned divisions within the Labour Party, it is they who receive the most attention. However, the Conservatives also feature briefly. Many of those addressing the Labour

Party's divisions drew a link between the renegotiations and/or the referendum and these divisions. Jeremy Thorpe (Lib) asserts that "the renegotiations were primarily for the benefit of the Labour Party and not for the country at large" (Hansard 1974–1975 889, col. 847) and that "the referendum is increasingly seen in the country to be a device to keep together the Labour Party" (ibid.:849). David Knox (C) also affirms that:

> There seems to be fairly general agreement on both sides of the House, with one or two exceptions—the Prime Minister is one—that from beginning to end they were a sham, more concerned with the internal affairs of the Labour Party than with the interests of Britain or of the European Economic Community. (ibid.:887)

Although this can be interpreted as a standard piece of knockabout party politics, it also shows the power of the European issue to weaken and divide political parties in the UK. Two panjandrums of the Conservative Party, Edward Heath and Margaret Thatcher, whilst agreeing with the Government on the issue of EEC membership, also take aim at the Labour Party's divisions. First, Thatcher notes that Wilson "has to rely more on his political opponents than on his alleged political friends to secure the decision which he considers right for Britain" (ibid.: 1021). Second, Heath invites the Prime Minister, with reference to the referendum, to "reflect on the old Chinese saying, 'Never lift a stone to drop on your own toe'" (ibid.:1276). It is easy to imagine the sound of teeth grinding as Ken Clarke advises David Cameron in similar terms…

The newspapers also devote some column inches to the Labour Party's travails: divided parties and disagreements always provide good copy. One editorial in *The Times* states that division in the Labour Party over the EEC "more frequently seems to be the reflection rather than the cause of other differences of philosophy and policy" (The Times 1975d). A second, entitled *Labour Divides on Europe*, notes that because the referendum "has already destroyed the formal political unity of the Labour Party and … many of the conventions which help to keep a party together," Wilson "will have to fight for his political life on the European issue" (The Times 1975b). Editorials in the *Daily Express* follow a similar line to *The Times*, with one asserting that "a referendum is merely a device for keeping the Labour Party together" (Daily Express 1975a). A second notes that the "charade of Britain's renegotiations" was "done to keep the Labour Party united" (Daily Express 1975d). The *Daily Mirror* also briefly addresses the issue of a divided Labour Party, worrying that "If the anti-Marketeers succeed in their aim, they will split the already divided Labour Party more deeply" (Daily Mirror 1975a). The *Daily Express*, in an editorial immediately before the referendum, addresses Conservative Party dynamics. The 4-June column takes a swipe at Edward du Cann, criticising as an "appalling accusation" his pronouncement that, were it not for ingrained loyalty, the Conservative Party would be split 50–50 on Europe (Daily Express 1975b).

This feature of the discourse is interesting given the charges of party division and criticism of Prime Minister Harold Wilson's attempts to hold his party together through renegotiation and referendum. These are charges and criticisms that might also be applied to David Cameron and his similar approach to the UK–EU relationship and similar party management issues. Indeed, Edward du Cann's accusation earlier would currently seem rather less appalling.

3.6   CHAPTER CONCLUSION

In drawing this chapter to a close, I observe that the pro-Marketeers held a somewhat stronger position in the discourse than the anti-Marketeers. This was particularly the case in the media discourse and in the campaign literature (where two of the three leaflets were in favour of EEC membership). The three major themes all had a relatively equal degree of importance in the discourse. There were clear tensions between issues of economy and sovereignty, with the prospect of EFTA membership being criticised by pro-Marketeers as a sacrifice of sovereignty. In terms of overall tone, the *Daily Express* editorial from the day of the referendum sums it up nicely, noting the importance of both hope and fear in taking the UK into the EEC. The editorial observes that the pro-Marketeers used fear, in particular, to good effect (Daily Express 1975c). An editorial from *The Times* cited earlier also talks about hopes and fears with regard to EEC membership (The Times 1975e). My analysis of the discourse would endorse the *Daily Express* editorial's view that the pro-Marketeers' case for EEC membership was largely based on fears: fears of economic meltdown, fears of unstable food supplies, and fears about the UK's place in the world. This lack of a positive case for EEC/EU membership is a phenomenon that persists currently. Other representations that have perpetuated are Eurosceptic fears of being subsumed and EFTA as a potential alternative. Finally, a point of interest from a reflectivist standpoint: the discourse often displayed consensus about "the reality" of a situation (e.g. loss/ transfer of sovereignty), but debate and disagreement over how this reality should be interpreted.

NOTES

1. I had originally intended to use the later debates on the Referendum Bill, but they proved to be more technical in nature, concentrating on how the referendum should be carried out. The White Paper debate aligned better with the arguments set out in the campaign literature and media discourse.
2. The debates I accessed on the Hansard website, copying the relevant material into a Word document before reading and analysing them. This also enabled searching for particular terms and provided the word count.
3. I cannot help but observe the repeated use of "the housewife" and "housewives" in the discourse. It is an interesting throwback, having today been replaced by the heuristic of "hard-working families."
4. Lord Justice Denning made this remark in the 1974 judgment *H.P. Bulmer Ltd v J. Bollinger SA*.

REFERENCES

Booker, C., & North, R. (2005). *The great deception: Can the European Union survive?* (2nd ed). London: Continuum. xii, 643 p. pp.

Britain in Europe Campaign. (1975). *Referendum on the European community, common market: Why you should vote yes*. London: Britain in Europe Campaign.

Daily Express. (1975a, January 24). Mr Wilson's price [Editorial]. *Daily Express*.

Daily Express. (1975b, June 4). The last stunt [Editorial]. *Daily Express*.

Daily Express. (1975c, June 5). The referendum—Act 1 [Editorial]. *Daily Express*.

Daily Express. (1975d, March 11). When to be inflexible [Editorial]. *Daily Express*.

Daily Mirror. (1975a, February 27). A decision for Britain [Editorial]. *Daily Mirror*.

Daily Mirror. (1975b, May 23). What's good for St Michael [Editorial]. *Daily Mirror*.

Diez, T. (2004). Europe's others and the return of geopolitics. *Cambridge Review of International Affairs, 17*(2), 319–335.

Ekman, I. (2005). In Norway, EU pros and cons (the cons still win). *The New York Times*. Retrieved February 5, 2014, from http://www.nytimes.com/2005/10/26/world/europe/26iht-norway.html?_r=0

Hansard. (1974–1975). *House of Commons Debates* (Vol. 889), Col. 821–961, 1020–150, 1243–371.

Harmsen, R., & Spiering, M. (2004). *Euroscepticism: Party politics, national identity and European integration.* European studies. Amsterdam: Rodopi. 290 p. pp.

Heffer, S. (2013, 29 March). The week the Fourth Reich began (without a shot being fired). *Daily Mail.*

HM Government. (1975). *Britain's new deal in Europe.* London: H.M.S.O. 15 p. pp.

Larsen, H. (1999). British and Danish European policies in the 1990s: A discourse approach. *European Journal of International Relations, 5*(4), 451–483.

Ludlow, N. P. (2015). Safeguarding british identity or betraying it? The role of British 'tradition'in the parliamentary great debate on EC membership, October 1971. *JCMS: Journal of Common Market Studies, 53*(1), 18–34.

Marcussen, M., Risse, T., Engelmann-Martin, D., Knopf, H. J., & Roscher, K. (1999). Constructing Europe? The evolution of French, British and German nation state identities. *Journal of European Public Policy, 6*(4), 614–633.

National Referendum Campaign. (1975). *Referendum on the European community, common market: Why you should vote no.* London: National Referendum Campaign.

Roberts, A. (1992). Evan Luard as a writer on international affairs. *Review of International Studies, 18*(1), 63–73.

Shapiro, M. J. (1989). Textualising global politics. In M. J. Shapiro & J. Der Derian (Eds.), *International/intertextual relations: Postmodern readings of World politics* (353 p.). Lexington, MA: Lexington.

The Economist. (2004). The Norwegian option. *The Economist.* Retrieved February 5, 2014, from http://www.economist.com/node/3262652

The Times. (1975a, February 27). A bill of rights against parliament [Editorial]. *The Times.*

The Times. (1975b, September 23). Budgeting For Waste [Editorial]. *The Times.*

The Times. (1975c, May 31). If in, we share the decisions: If out, they are made for us [Editorial]. *The Times.*

The Times. (1975d, March 10). Last fence in Dublin [Editorial]. *The Times.*

The Times. (1975e, April 31). Sovereignty [Editorial]. *The Times.*

van Randwyck, H. (2011). *EFTA or the EU.* London: The Bruges Group.

Young, H. (1998). *This blessed plot: Britain and Europe from Churchill to Blair.* London: Macmillan. xiv, 558, 24 p. of plates pp.

CHAPTER 4

The British Discourse on Europe 1992–1993: Major and the Maastricht "Bastards"

Abstract This chapter provides a detailed analysis of the febrile debates over the UK's ratification of the Maastricht Treaty. This period is of interest given the emergence of divisions within the Conservative Party, which persist to this day. The major themes in the discourse are identified as *Centralisation, Federalisation, and Subsidiarity; Economic and Monetary Union;* and *Sovereignty and Democracy.* These themes show some continuity from 1975, with Sovereignty and Democracy once again present as a major theme. Clear definitions of self and other are present, with repeated representation of an island self at threat from an anti-democratic other based in Europe.

Keywords Maastricht Treaty • Federalism • Subsidiarity • Sovereignty • Democracy • Economic and Monetary Union

This chapter looks at the debates over the UK's ratification of the Maastricht Treaty. Prior to Maastricht, Margaret Thatcher had eventually been brought down as Prime Minister by her intransigence over Europe, and was replaced by the more emollient John Major. Major's tenure as Prime Minister came to be defined by his loss of authority during the debates over ratification of the Maastricht Treaty. With reference to the research questions, this chapter gives an opportunity to begin assessing *changes* and *continuities* across the first two periods under analysis. As mentioned later in the text, immigration makes its first appearance as a minor theme in the discourse. The debates on economic and monetary union (EMU) are also of contemporary interest given the ongoing attempts to solve the crisis in the Eurozone.

The Maastricht Treaty (formally referred to as The Treaty on European Union) was signed on 7 February 1992, and came into force on 1 November 1993. The Treaty made provision for the creation of three "pillars" of the EU: the European Communities, a Common Foreign and Security Policy (CFSP), and cooperation on Justice and Home Affairs (JHA) matters. It also included provision for common European citizenship, expanding the role of the European Parliament, EMU, and a Social Protocol. The Treaty was implemented in UK law through the European Communities (Amendment) Act 1993.

The domestic politics of the UK form an essential part of the context for the ratification of the Maastricht Treaty, though international issues, particularly those of a financial nature, also need to be considered. Major's performance at the Maastricht negotiations was widely regarded as a success, both by media commentators at the time and by subsequent historians. Hugo Young (1998:433) describes "the ecstatic reception the conquering hero received on his return from the Netherlands." Booker and North (2005:336) agree, noting that "the newspapers were almost unanimous in praise of what the *Daily Telegraph* called 'Major's success at Maastricht.'" The Prime Minister had secured opt-outs for the United Kingdom on EMU and on the Social Protocol. Hugo Young (1998:435) notes that the image of competence built up by Major during these negotiations played into 1992s general election campaign. Despite Labour beginning the election campaign as strong favourites, the Conservatives won, and John Major returned as Prime Minister, albeit with a small majority of 21 MPs (see Kettle 2005).

The European Communities (Amendment) Bill was introduced to Parliament soon after the general election. The Labour leadership and Liberal Democrats, whilst generally supportive of the Maastricht Treaty, were critical of the Government for opting out of the Social Protocol and the provisions on EMU. A number of Conservative MPs were strongly opposed to the Treaty, including William Cash, who was soon to be seen as leader of the Tory Eurosceptics and a particularly painful thorn in John Major's side. It is worth noting that, whilst the majority of those who displayed disloyalty to the Prime Minister were backbenchers without ministerial office, the Cabinet was also divided on the issue. In particular, there were the three Ministers who John Major famously referred to as "bastards" for their disloyalty over Europe: Peter Lilley, Michael Portillo, and John Redwood. Describing this forcefully, Fontana and Parsons (2015:97) note that "striking Thatcher down made her (or rather her ideas) more powerful than her rivals could have possibly imagined."

The first Danish referendum on 2 June that rejected the Maastricht Treaty caused Major to delay detailed consideration of amendments to his Parliamentary Bill. During this period of delay, huge pressure was put on a number of currencies within the European Exchange Rate Mechanism (ERM; the semi-pegged system of currency exchange rates designed as a precursor to EMU). The pressure on the pound caused humiliation for Major and his Chancellor of the Exchequer, Norman Lamont. On 17 September 1992, the Government was forced to suspend its membership of the ERM and devalue the pound. Black Wednesday, as it came to be known, destroyed the Government's economic credibility, weakened Major as Prime Minister, and strengthened those opposed to the Maastricht Treaty (see Booker and North 2005:346–7; Young 1998:440–1).

The debates on the Bill resumed in November and, after many hours of debate and many hundreds of amendments tabled by William Cash and other Eurosceptics, they reached a final crescendo on 22 July 1993. On this day the Government faced two crucial votes related to the Social Protocol, with Conservative rebels likely to side with Labour and the Liberal Democrats to cause a major defeat for the Government. The first vote was a dead heat, with the Speaker of the House of Commons placing her deciding vote in favour of the Government. The second vote was a defeat for the Government and led to calls for John Major's resignation. The following day, the Social Protocol was debated again.[1] The Prime Minister framed the debate and subsequent vote as matters of confidence in the Government, stating that a defeat would cause him to call a general election. Baker et al. (1994:44) describe this as a threat of "electoral Mutually Assured Destruction." The dismal poll ratings of the Conservative Party likely convinced the rebels to value their attachment to their Parliamentary seats more highly than their Euroscepticism: only one Conservative MP rebelled this time. The Government therefore won the vote and the Maastricht Treaty was ratified, though at great cost to the Prime Minister and the unity of his party. As Booker and North (2005:354) observe, "Major won the day by 39 votes. Around him stood the wreckage of the Conservative Party."

The discourse analysed here is drawn from the period of this legislation's journey from Bill to Act, from 20 May 1992 to 23 July 1993, and includes the following:

- Parliamentary debates on the European Communities (Amendment) Bill. The debates analysed are the second reading of the Bill and the debate on the Social Protocol. The second reading debate is the first major debate on the Bill and addresses the major issues at stake with the legislation. In the case of this legislation, this debate took place over two days and nights from 20 to 21 May 1992. The debate on the Social Protocol took place at the end of the legislative process (on 23 July 1993) as a result of many Conservative MPs rebelling against the Government. These two debates amount to over 225,000 words.[2]
- Newspaper editorials from 1992 to 1993 that mention the Maastricht Treaty. More than 80 editorials from *The Times* and the *Daily Mail* were analysed.

Overall, there are three main positions observable in the discourse: Eurosceptics opposed to Maastricht, Government voices seeking ratification of the treaty, and those arguing that the Government was not pro-European enough. Without having the benefit of campaign literature to assist in identifying the important themes, I turned this time to the opening speeches of the Prime Minister and Leader of the Opposition in the European Communities (Amendment) Bill debates. The two speeches, in particular that of the Prime Minister, address the major issues which I term *Centralisation, Federalisation, and Subsidiarity*; *Economic and Monetary Union*; and *Sovereignty and Democracy*. Both the speeches address all three major issues of these themes and the more minor theme of *the Social Protocol*. Only the Prime Minister mentions the other minor theme of *Freedom of Movement and Immigration*, although it is addressed through the rest of the Parliamentary debates and in the editorials. In high-level terms, these themes show some continuity from 1975, with Sovereignty and Democracy once again present as a major theme. Some change is also clear, with, for example, Centralisation, Federalisation, and Subsidiarity and Freedom of Movement and Immigration newly present in the discourse. I note that the discourse is more interwoven than in 1975, with multiple linkages clear between all three major themes. Again, a brief analysis of *Portrayals of Party Division* is included before the chapter concludes.

Before moving to the first major theme, I note that each Parliamentary contributor whose party allegiance is not obvious (e.g. John Major) has once again an abbreviated label after their name. These are L – Labour, C – Conservative, LD – Liberal Democrat, and UUP – Ulster Unionist Party. Where appropriate, I group quotes from similar sources (e.g. Labour Eurosceptics).

4.1   Centralisation, Federalisation, and Subsidiarity

One major theme present in the discourse encompasses arguments on the theme of Centralisation, Federalisation, and Subsidiarity. These three key positions are visible in the Parliamentary debate: those who felt that the Maastricht Treaty and its provision for subsidiarity[3] would put a stop to centralisation/federalisation (mainly Government voices), those concerned that it would do exactly the opposite (Eurosceptic voices), and finally those who argued in favour of a federal model for Europe. These three positions represent the Treaty's effects on centralisation as a turning point, a con trick, and as an unwelcome challenge to federalism, respectively. Starting with the first of these positions, John Major is the most important voice. He makes a clear statement in favour of subsidiarity in his opening speech:

> Many in this House and throughout the country have expressed anxiety that decision making in the Community is becoming too centralised. In fact, many of the issues which are most problematic for us—I shall talk about some of them later—arise from the application of the original treaty of Rome, not the Maastricht Treaty. The Maastricht Treaty marks the point at which, for the first time, we have begun to reverse that centralising trend. We have moved decision taking back towards the member states in areas where Community law need not and should not apply. ... We have secured a legally binding text on subsidiarity. (Hansard 1992–1993a:208 col. 265–6)

Pollack (2000:526) endorses this perspective, stating that "the subsidiarity provision constituted a victory for the hard-line positions of the German Länder and the British government." The Foreign Secretary, Douglas Hurd, makes similar points, arguing that "Maastricht was an important step away from an increasingly centralised, and therefore arthritic, Community towards a new Europe in which Britain has a central place" (Hansard 1992–1993a:208 col. 519). The *Daily Mail* follows a similar line to the Government, noting on 30 April that "The momentum towards an ever more federal Community no longer seems to have such a sense of inevitability. It may be that posterity will see Maastricht, not as a staging post on the way to a United States of Europe, but rather as the high water mark for the ambitions of those who dream that dream" (Daily Mail 1992c). These quotes seek to frame subsidiarity as a turning of the tide against centralisation. In supporting this line, Tony Marlow (C) harks back to a period of threat to the UK:

> Maastricht was a brilliant tactical victory, but the forces of federalism—artificially camouflaged during ratification—have yet to be banished. The heart of Bonaparte still beats in many breasts … The House should dedicate itself to the fight against Bonapartism. This should be the trumpet, the clarion call, the beginning of a march to a second Waterloo. (Hansard 1992–1993a:208 col. 345)

This is an interesting and emotive use of history, linking those who desire federalism with Napoleon Bonaparte's desire to conquer Europe. Like with references to the Second World War, drawing upon Napoleonic metaphor frames the European issue as one of threat, invasion, and autocracy. In slightly more restrained fashion, Michael Colvin (C) also salutes the Prime Minister and Foreign Secretary, "whose delicate political and diplomatic strategy has mitigated most of Mr. Delors' federalist plans, while avoiding any break with our continental partners" (ibid.:430). Colvin goes on to assert that "Last December's treaty will be seen as a turning point in the history of the Community. The British Government have succeeded in tilting the European agenda in their direction, away from creeping centralisation" (ibid.:432). Those in favour of subsidiarity represent the issue as a victory over the rest of Europe, thwarting their "federalist plans." This oppositional attitude is clearly based on differentiation and a sense of the UK being a lone voice against the centralising desires of the rest of Europe.

Those taking a more strongly Eurosceptic line and arguing that subsidiarity would do little to combat federalism were, for the most part, Conservative backbenchers. Teddy Taylor (C) affirms that:

the Prime Minister said that he interpreted the Maastricht Treaty as a transfer of matters back to the nations. Not one of the other 11 Prime Ministers
in the European Community would interpret that agreement in that way. ...
I can assure the House that the projection is towards federalism and a united
states of Europe. (ibid.:327–8)

Other Conservative Eurosceptics, worried about federalism and critical
of subsidiarity, develop this theme. William Cash (C) asserts that "The
Bill is about the future government and democracy of Europe and of the
United Kingdom. The gravitational pull in the treaty—which is endorsed
by the Bill—would take us, indeed, drag us, into a federal Europe"
(ibid.:312), and that "I believe that the principle of subsidiarity is a con
trick" (ibid.:314). This perspective is supported by Peter Hordern (C),
who claims that

> The love of the French for Cartesian logic has bred a race of functionaries
> certain that they are always right; of such is Mr. Delors. In France, this takes
> the form of protectionism; in Brussels it takes the form of deepening the
> European Community before broadening it. (ibid.:330)

This piece of differentiation leads Hordern to conclude "That means
that Brussels will take every opportunity to centralise power, convinced
that that is in the best interests of the Community" (ibid.). James Cran
(C) fears "that the principle of subsidiarity is no more than a fig leaf"
(ibid.:444). Iain Duncan-Smith (later to become Conservative leader)
states that "we remain locked into what I see as a continuing progression
towards a European super-state" (ibid.:354). An editorial in *The Times*,
meanwhile, worries that "federalist fervour still burns in the hearts of many
European politicians" (The Times 1993b). Here, we can see subsidiarity
represented as a "fig leaf" and "con trick," the French as "a race of functionaries," and concerns about "federalist fervour," centralising power in
Brussels, and the prospect of "a European super-state." Taken together,
the quotations show a clear differentiation between the UK and a centralising, federalist European other. The quotes demonstrate a sense of
British exceptionalism, in that these Eurosceptics believe that it should be
the responsibility of the UK to fight what George Gardiner (C) describes
as the "shadow of federalism" (Hansard 1992–1993a:208 col. 369).
Timothy Garton Ash describes this sense of exceptionalism as "A story
of separateness, starting with the geographical separation of the offshore

island from the mainland, but then, following the end of the Hundred Years War, of political separation" (2001:5). The comments from Peter Hordern are particularly strong, linking French "protectionism" with a desire to "centralise power" in Brussels. Hordern's reference here to "a race of functionaries" being "bred" is a clear and somewhat unpleasant example of differentiation.

The Labour Party too had voices critical of the Treaty and worried about federalism. Peter Shore (L) asserts that "We have to face the fact that, almost from the start, our neighbours have wanted a federal union on the continent of Europe, and the British people have never wanted that" (Hansard 1992–1993a:208 col. 283). Shore here clearly draws a distinction between "the British people" opposed to federal union and continental "neighbours" in favour of such a union. Tony Benn (L) makes reference to both World Wars in explaining his opposition to the "enforced centralisation" of the Treaty:

> We have had two world wars. Everyone in Britain lost people in them. I lost an uncle in the first world war and a brother and friends in the second world war. Everyone wants a peaceful Europe. But the House should not think that enforced centralisation produces peace. Look at Bosnia-Herzegovina, at Slovenia and Croatia. One cannot run capitalism from Brussels in the way that people tried to run communism from Moscow. (ibid.:319)

As in the previous chapter, world war is employed here to justify Euroscepticism. The ethnic conflict in Yugoslavia mentioned by Benn is also referred to by the Conservative Eurosceptic Christopher Gill: "If we consider the course of world history, we see that the failure of federalism is well documented—in Africa, Canada, the Caribbean, Russia, and now in western Europe, in Yugoslavia. We are foolish to ignore the lessons of history" (ibid.:415). These references to conflict are noteworthy. On one level, given that conflict is an extreme method for changing/maintaining social boundaries, bringing it into a debate about the transfer of authority to Europe is, perhaps, to be expected. However, it does say something about the terms of the debate whenever the issue of European unity is consistently framed through reference to previous conflicts and a range of military metaphors. These examples show how politicians use history, sometimes in extreme ways, to frame contemporary policy proposals.

Tam Dalyell (L), in contrast, argues in favour of centralism with reference to contemporary challenges:

As a concept, "centralism" is a bit of a dirty word, but how other than through a centralist approach does one approach the problem of the ozone layer ... How else other than on a central European basis can we do anything about the rain forests? And how else can we do anything about marine pollution? The air that we breathe is common. If we want to do something about chlorofluorocarbons in the third world and about skin cancer, we must do it on a European basis, or on an even wider basis than that. (ibid.:342)

This approach is also taken by Harry Barnes (L) when arguing against subsidiarity and in favour of federalism: "Subsidiarity is a fog within which decision making passes to the more undemocratic institutions of the EC. The answer is to make those institutions as democratic as possible. ... We need a federal, social and democratic Europe" (ibid.:427). It is possible to observe a link being drawn to issues of sovereignty and democracy (addressed in more detail below) by the proponents of federalism, in that they are in favour of pooling sovereignty through a "federal, social, and democratic Europe."

This theme has encompassed three broad positions. First were those who agreed with the Government that the principle of subsidiarity had "turned the tide" against centralisation and federalisation. Second were those who represented subsidiarity as a "con trick," claiming that centralisation and federalisation would increase apace as a result of Maastricht. Third were those arguing in favour of federalism in the belief that Maastricht did not go far enough in this regard. The second position was, if not dominant, then certainly the loudest and most emotive. The use of previous military threat, be it from Napoleon or Hitler, is noteworthy in that such use seeks to frame the issue as one involving an external, dictatorial invader. Those who took this Eurosceptic view linked themselves with "the people" and differentiated themselves from those—generally based in/allied with Brussels—who desired a federal Europe. It is also worth noting that *both* the Government line and the more strongly Eurosceptic voices based their arguments on differentiation from the rest of Europe. The Government argument was one of having successfully resisted federalist plans from the continent, whilst the Eurosceptics like Taylor and Cash argued that these federalists remained in the ascendant and thus continued to be a threat to the UK. Those distinguishing a British self from a Continental other thus hold a dominant position here.

4.2   Economic and Monetary Union

Given that the Maastricht Treaty made provision for the highly significant issue of a currency union in Europe, it is unsurprising that this issue forms a major theme in the British discourse, encompassing debates about the significance of the UK's opt-out from EMU, and the general implications of such a union. These debates are of contemporary significance given the ongoing crisis in the Eurozone. It is also interesting to note a degree of continuity from the pro-/anti-Market debates of 1975 here. Those who are critical of economic and monetary union on the political left employ similar arguments here as were employed during the referendum debates. The Prime Minister once again claims success for the results of his negotiations:

> The treaty also sets exactly the framework that we want for economic and monetary union. It provides a commitment to open and competitive markets, a commitment that this country has sought for years and that many felt might never be available from our Community partners. ... Above all, it contains an absolute right for the United Kingdom—its Parliament—to decide later, and at a time of its own choosing, whether or not it wishes to move to the third stage of economic and monetary union. (ibid.:269)

Major here displays a commitment to free market economics through reference to "open and competitive markets" and "price stability," celebrating the attainment of "exactly the framework that we want" in this regard. The Prime Minister subtly differentiates on the basis of economic policy here, in that he claims that the liberal approach he secured was thought to be impossible to obtain from other countries in the EEC. Major also gives a nod towards parliamentary sovereignty in affirming that Parliament retains an "absolute right" to decide on the UK's involvement in a single currency. The Labour leader Neil Kinnock is, however, critical of this. He argues that "The opt-out over economic and monetary union was contrived by the Prime Minister to mollify the former leader of the Conservative party and her followers" (ibid.:276). Kinnock goes on to speak in detail about the UK's increasing economic interdependence within Europe, concluding that:

> Given that exports account for one third of our gross domestic product, a large proportion of our production capacity and of British jobs depend on sales in the Community. That basic consideration should guide Government

policy on economic and monetary union. The growing interdependence to which I referred will make it essential for the British Government to play a full and constructive role in the process of achieving the economic and monetary union that is under way. (ibid.:278)

Liberal Democrat leader Paddy Ashdown echoes Kinnock's criticism of the opt-out, stating that:

We all pay a high price for that piece of sticking plaster. We pay for it in that we shall not have the influence that we should have over the shape of the monetary union institutions. We pay for it in that our opportunity to have the European central bank located in Britain has been blown away. (ibid.:298)

Derek Enright (L) argues in favour of EMU in a manner that echoes the pro-Marketeer arguments in 1975, "As a result of coming together and pooling our sovereignties, we shall gain infinitely more sovereignty over the pound and economic policy than we have at present" (ibid.:311).

This argument found opposition from Eurosceptics in both the Conservative and Labour parties. Despite the UK's opt-out, these MPs raised concerns about EMU and its potential impact on the UK. Beginning with the Conservatives, William Cash claims that "The reality is that these independent, unelected bankers are to be given the surrogate power of government in Europe. That is absolutely and totally unacceptable" (ibid.:315). Other Conservative backbenchers also link EMU with loss of sovereignty, damage to democracy, and the threat of European federalism. George Gardiner (C) notes that "Maastricht was a disappointment all round for the federalists. However, they were halted but not defeated, and their hope is that the provisions on a single currency will bring economic, and hence political, federation into being in due course" (ibid.:368). Christopher Gill (C) considers

the Maastricht Treaty to be a poor deal for British democracy because it ends the sovereign right of the Westminster Parliament to tax and to spend. It is a poor deal for the British people, because their democratically elected representatives will increasingly be seen to have had their influence over the nation's affairs neutered. (ibid.:414–5)

Finally, Sir Michael Spicer (C) is convinced that "There can be no question but that a move towards a single currency is a move towards a federal united states of Europe." (ibid.:570). Once again, we can observe classic Eurosceptic fears (a united states of Europe, unelected figures taking power from Parliament) being invoked to frame the EEC negatively. The *Daily Mail* also has a sceptical take on the prospects for EMU:

> For, in years to come, Britain's taxpayers will have to hand over to the Poor Four (Spain, Portugal, Greece and Ireland) more than this Tory Government bargained for. The spectacle of Felipe Gonzalez acting the able-bodied beggar on behalf of the relatively prosperous Spanish people is enough to turn the stomach on a planet where poverty, disease and starvation are all too real. That is pork barrel politics. Support pledged for favours given... 'I will swallow the Danish opt-out clauses, Senor, if you will grease my palm'. (Daily Mail 1992b)

The editorial employs ethical dimensions of identity to differentiate "Britain's taxpayers" from "the able bodied beggar" of Spain's Prime Minister. The imagined quotation appears xenophobic. *The Times* has several editorials critical of the ERM and the prospects of EMU. One argues that the Labour Party sees the ERM "as a way of introducing German-style social controls and French-style industrial interventionism by the back door" (The Times 1992b). A second editorial states, arguably with some foresight, that

> The Bundesbank's obsession with reducing inflation at the expense of growth and prosperity, and its only grudging response to pressure from politicians, are merely a foretaste of what life would be like under European monetary union with an independent central bank. (The Times 1992d)

A third editorial makes a link between federalism and monetary union, asserting that "attempts to create a federal Europe by the monetary back door will continue to wreak economic havoc" (The Times 1993a). *The Times* frames ERM as potentially enabling unwanted impositions from Europe by the "back door." Spatial dimensions of identity are combined to raise the spectre of unwelcome "German-style social controls" and "French-style industrial interventionism."

Labour sceptics of EMU are similarly critical to their Conservative counterparts. For example, Denzil Davies (L) also argues against the provisions through reference to "undemocratic Community institutions." He affirms that "The economic and monetary union proposals in the treaty entail a massive, substantial shift of power over money and our fiscal and economic policy from democratically elected Government and Parliament to undemocratic Community institutions" (Hansard 1992–1993a:208 col. 300). This differentiation between a democratic British self and undemocratic European is followed by other Labour backbenchers. For example, Nigel Spearing (L) criticises the lack of democratic accountability: "If Europe is not to be dominated by bankers for bankers, there must be some form of democratic accountability. I cannot see that in the treaty or in the aspirations of those who support it" (ibid.:336). Austin Mitchell (L) is concerned that "we will unleash economic forces that will subject Europe to a common economic misery under a dominant German economy" (ibid.:357–8), whilst Ron Leighton (L) argues that "The objective is to squeeze all of us into a single currency run by an unelected, unaccountable central bank" (ibid.:548–9). Clive Betts (L) is critical from a perspective of loss of sovereignty: "To have an independent bank that is unaccountable under any circumstances to any elected representatives is to undermine the sovereignty of people who cannot influence vital monetary and interest rate policies" (ibid.:413). These Labour figures make much of issues of democracy here, asserting that EMU would lead to a loss of democratic accountability to unelected figures in Europe.

It is interesting to note the similarities in approach between sceptics from the Conservative right and Labour left, given their very different outlooks on matters of economic policy. Both groups argue against EMU via notions of self, which include reference to democracy, sovereignty, and "the British people." Baker's work on elite discourse and public opinion observes in this regard "a growing popular perception of a damaging loss of parliamentary sovereignty implied by currency union" (Baker 2002:19). I also note that a number of the quotes mentioned earlier (e.g. Austin Mitchell's portent of "common economic misery under a dominant German economy") would not look out of place in a contemporary debate on the Eurozone crisis. In summing up the debate, the Chancellor of the Exchequer acknowledges some of these backbench concerns:

A single currency could not work if Governments pursued irresponsible, lax fiscal policies. But having a general fiscal rule is not the same as surrendering control over the levels of taxation and expenditure. It is, however, clear that a single currency—here I approach the point made by my hon. Friend the Member for Stafford [William Cash] —involves removing control of monetary policy from national Governments. The treaty proposes that it should be handed, not to a European executive, Government or state, but to a monetary authority independent of all national Governments. (Hansard 1992–1993a:208 col.589)

Again, these comments resonate when viewed from a perspective informed by the Eurozone crisis. In summarising this theme, I note that the voices critical of EMU hold a strong position within the discourse. Again, their arguments are framed through differentiation of the British self from a Continental other. In framing the issue in this way, the sceptics repeatedly represent European institutions as undemocratic and unaccountable. As mentioned earlier, both Labour and Conservative MPs use such arguments in justifying their opposition to EMU. The similarity of their approach here is striking.

4.3   Sovereignty and Democracy

The third major theme of sovereignty and democracy is a pervasive element of the discourse. The other two major themes also mention issues of sovereignty and democracy. Yet, more continuity from the 1975 debates is clear here, because both those fearing loss of sovereignty and damage to democracy, and those welcoming the pooling of said sovereignty, argue with agnate tone and content from 1975. One difference from 1975 is the presence of Government voices attempting to find a middle course, arguing that the Maastricht Treaty restricts loss of sovereignty and safeguards democracy. The Prime Minister approaches this challenge via a broad perspective:

> We in this generation have the opportunity and the responsibility for managing the biggest transition to democracy in our continent in its entire history. There will be many means at our disposal for achieving that, both national and international. I have no doubt that crucial among them is the European Community. If we had to point towards one endeavour that can consolidate European democracy, boost our collective European economic prosperity and enhance our collective international influence, it is the European Community. (ibid.:273)

The Foreign Secretary takes a more detailed approach, stating that:

> The European Parliament plays an important part in reinforcing the efforts of national Parliaments and contributing to filling any democratic deficit. We supported changes in Maastricht to give the directly elected European

Parliament more control over the Commission and the scrutiny of the Community's finances. (ibid.:516)

Hurd goes on to assert that "The treaty of Maastricht reinforces the position of national Parliaments, which, as far as I am aware, is a new development in the history of European treaties" (ibid.:517). Here, we can see two key Government figures arguing that democracy on both European and national levels will be consolidated and reinforced by the European Community and the Maastricht Treaty. Both appeal to this being a unique moment in history. These are examples of Foucault's (2004:66) assertion that the "practice of recounting history [is] related to the rituals of power," in that both appeal to history in supporting their case for Maastricht ratification. The *Daily Mail* also follows a middle path here, noting that:

> The claim, that if we reject Maastricht, Britain—starved of trade with the continent—will disappear into offshore oblivion, is grossly exaggerated. The sceptics' nightmare vision that Maastricht will lead to a vast, centrally controlled European superstate, swallowing up national identities, is similarly distorted. The truth probably lies somewhere in the middle. Maastricht will dilute national sovereignty. It could also, stripped of its interfering bureaucracy, bring great advantages to Britain. (Daily Mail 1992d)

Tony Benn (L) meanwhile recounts history when setting out his fears for the executive gaining the upper hand over Parliament. He states that "The Prime Minister ... can agree to laws in Brussels at the Council of Ministers, which take precedence over laws passed by the House. For the first time since 1649, the prerogative controls the House, instead of the House controlling the prerogative" (Hansard 1992–1993a:208 col. 268). He later notes that:

> We have misled the British people about the meaning of the Community from the point of view of our own Parliament. The House is now governed by the royal prerogative for the first time since 1649. Over the centuries, Parliament has grabbed back prerogatives from the Crown—even that one on the security services, inadequate as it was—and put matters in statute. Now any Minister can use the prerogative to encompass and control Parliament. ... It reduces the House of Commons to a municipal body which can be rate-capped and fined. (ibid.:317)

This quote shows Benn making a claim of facticity with regard to the legislature losing out to the executive. Of course, concerns about the "democratic deficit" are far from unique to the UK (see for example Harmsen and Spiering 2004). This notion of a democratic deficit is addressed by both Eurosceptics like Benn and pro-Europeans like Paddy Ashdown. Ashdown states that "The great deficiency of the Maastricht Treaty is the democratic deficit. The institutions that we are building will not be accountable to the European Parliament or to those who elect Members of the European Parliament" (Hansard 1992–1993a:208 col.297). This line of argument is supported by the Labour MP Geoff Hoon and the Conservative MP Mark Robinson. Robinson agrees that the issue of the democratic deficit is unresolved: "If we give our people the impression that they are being governed by unelected bureaucrats from Brussels, we will create and store up future dangers for the Community's development due to the political forces that will be unleashed" (ibid.:363). Geoff Hoon argues that Maastricht "will do little … to make the European Commission subject to democratic control. Similarly, the decisions of the Council of Ministers, meeting in secret, are rarely subject to democratic scrutiny" (ibid.:366). Both are critical, whether in terms of "meeting in secret" or of "unelected bureaucrats" and assert that the remedy for this is enhanced democracy at the European level. These worries are also displayed in an editorial in *The Times*, which observes that "the recurrent nightmare of every British prime minister is a continental cabal whose decisions would determine British politics and the economy" (The Times 1993a). The metaphor of a "Continental cabal"—secretive, prone to intrigue—is a noteworthy piece of "othering" via conceptual intertextuality.

Others who share these criticisms are markedly less optimistic about the prospects of European-level democracy. Sir Michael Spicer (C) warns of "the threat to our own peculiar—I say that in an admiring way—form of democracy, a form that is not, for example, shared in France. Compared to the British Parliament, the French Assembly does not count for a fig" (ibid.:570). Once more we see negative differentiation, with the British Parliament placed higher in the pantheon of democratic institutions than the French Assembly by Spicer. Tony Marlow (C) makes another colourful contribution, redolent with imagery of danger and threat:

> "We have been cheated, swindled and mugged by the self-same institutions that this very day are grovelling on their knees for us to give them more of our powers. Having lost our innocence and our wallets, does it not seem

a little perverse to venture again so soon on to the dark back streets of Brussels?" (ibid.:344)

Michael Lord (C) also employs emotive imagery of the UK as "an island nation" in his appeal: "We shall be voting on our country's identity and on our right to govern ourselves as an island nation" (ibid.:438). This quote shows an explicit link between foreign policy (the UK's relationship with Europe) and "our country's identity": Lord seeks to frame the vote on Maastricht ratification as one that will define the future identity and independence of the UK.

Labour concerns about sovereignty and democracy are also strongly present in the discourse: another element of continuity from 1975. Llew Smith (L) argues that Maastricht represents "a move away from democracy, devolution of power and accountable government to decisions being made by those who have never had the courage to stand for election" (ibid.:352–3). George Stevenson (L) reinforces this by stating that Maastricht "certainly does not establish any basis for real democracy over a European Community that is increasingly dominated by an unaccountable Commission and a secretive Council of Ministers" (ibid.:376). Peter Hain (L) and Austin Mitchell (L) make a link between loss of democratic sovereignty and economic issues in a manner similar to their anti-Marketeer forebears. Peter Hain affirms that "capital has gone European but labour has not. Transnationals now dominate the European economy. Financial deregulation has made it very difficult, if not impossible, within nation states to exert any serious democratic accountability" (ibid.:408). Austin Mitchell states that:

If this regime goes ahead, if a monetarist regime is fixed on Europe, the people will demonstrate an increasing frustration because their vote will count for nothing. .... In that situation, politics will turn sour. People unable to influence politicians, unable to reduce unemployment through political action, unable to use the power of democratic government over the power of money, will turn against immigrants, each other and everything that is better, altruistic and good in our society. There will be sourness. As the cake contracts, people will compete more bitterly and more fiercely for a share of that shrinking cake. That is not the sort of society that I am in politics to build. I am not in politics to make Europe fit to be ruled by central bankers, uncontrolled by the democratic power of the people. (ibid.:360)

Again, the quote from Austin Mitchell resonates strongly in the current European troika,[4] austerity, and large-scale youth unemployment. The prediction he makes regarding anti-immigrant opinion is also apposite. The inter-linked nature of the debate is clear here, with—as in 1975—economic issues featuring heavily in the arguments about sovereignty and democracy. There are clear examples of differentiation here, with ethical and spatial dimensions of identity being used to invoke a sense of something being inflicted on "the British people"/"ordinary citizen." For example, reference is made to loss of innocence on the "dark back streets of Brussels," loss of economic sovereignty to Europe, and that a "monetarist regime" is "not the sort of society that I am in politics to build." Those sceptical about European unity continue to represent a British self at threat from an anti-democratic, unaccountable, and secretive Continental other.

Like in the previous chapter, there are those who are more relaxed at the prospect of losing sovereignty to Europe. Tony Banks (L) asserts that "I am not worried about losing sovereignty … we are moving towards supranational organisations. Nationalism is a curse—we can see the effects of it in eastern Europe and we can now do something about it in western Europe" (ibid.:568). Conflict is prayed in aid, this time in favour of, rather than against, supranationalism. This once again demonstrates the importance of interpretation and backs up the idea that history—particularly in the hands of politicians—has as much or more to do with the present as the past. Robert Wareing (L) affirms that "On the doorsteps during the general election campaign, I heard not one suggestion—I doubt whether other hon. Members differ from me—that my constituents were worried about sovereignty" (ibid.:379). Finally, Brian Sedgemore (L) states that:

> We are meeting in this historic debate to confess that we now accept that sovereignty is a myth, that national independence is an illusion and that a love of parliamentary democracy is the fashionable excuse of those who so long for yesterday that they cannot face tomorrow. Tonight, we begin to draw a veil over parliamentary democracy as we have known it since 1832; tomorrow, we begin to unveil a new democracy. Our powerful, over-arching and over-centralised system of government is about to give way to a devolved European pluralism. (ibid.:571)

We can observe temporal dimensions of identity employed here, with those in favour of the nation state and Parliamentary democracy painted as anachronistic by Labour MPs Sedgemore and Banks. Wareing asserts that it is in fact those who are concerned about loss of sovereignty who are out of touch with the electorate. These voices occupy a relatively minor position in the discourse, particularly when compared to the Eurosceptics.

In concluding, I refer to another interesting quote from Brian Sedgemore, who states that "in Britain, we understand political theory so little that we easily confuse notions of sovereignty, identity and account-ability. In our confusion, we fear the French, the Italians, the Greeks and, above all, the Germans" (Hansard 1992–1993a:208 col. 572). This appears a reasonable summation of the Eurosceptic arguments, and the point Sedgemore makes about fear is important: it is a consistent fea-ture of the discourse. The Eurosceptic representation of the EEC as anti-democratic and unaccountable is dominant and employs much emotive rhetoric. Whilst I will return to this issue towards the end of this book, I note for now Delanty's statement in his article *Fear of Others: Social Exclusion and the European Crisis of Solidarity* that "Fear of others and anxieties about the future have emerged as potent social forces in contem-porary society. The result is a crisis of European solidarity, along with a wider crisis of collective purpose" (2008:676).

4.4   FREEDOM OF MOVEMENT AND IMMIGRATION

Debates about the implications of common European citizenship, free-dom of movement, and immigration form a minor theme. These debates took in internal controls (i.e. focused on movement within the European Community) and third-country immigration from outside the European Community. The Prime Minister states that:

> All of us in this country live daily with the evils of terrorism and drug smug-gling. No one doubts that we have to control immigration, in the best inter-ests of everyone who lives in this country. ... For most of our partners, the idea of an open frontier does not mean that there should be no limitations on what goods and people travel from one country to another. It reflects the fact that they cannot control these matters at the frontier and have therefore devised internal controls to do so.
>
> Our practice is different by virtue of our island status. Experience has shown us that control at the frontier gives us the best possible chance of containing smuggling, terrorism and illegal immigration. We accept the right of Community citizens to move freely between member states, but we must, as we agreed under the Single European Act, keep the controls that

we consider necessary to control immigration from third-world countries and to combat terrorism, crime and trafficking in drugs. That means that we must retain frontier controls, and we intend to do so. (ibid.:270–1)

The first analytical observation to be drawn from this quotation is the juxtaposition of "the evils of terrorism and drug smuggling" with the need to "control immigration." This phenomenon has been widely observed, with Huysmans (2000:752) noting that "migration has been increasingly presented as a threat to public order, cultural identity, and domestic labour market stability." Huysmans goes on to conclude that "This raises questions about how the development of a common migration policy feeds into the wider politics of belonging … connected to membership of the national and European community" (ibid.:771). The second observation is Major's claim to exceptionalism on the basis of the "island status" of the UK. Major accepts the principle of freedom of movement of those within the community, though argues in favour of frontier controls on the basis of threats of terrorism and crime.

Other Conservative MPs argue along similar lines. Kenneth Baker states that "the thing that is destabilising the Governments of European country after European country is migratory flows" (Hansard 1992–1993a:208 col. 291). Dame Angela Rumbold (C) links immigration to employment and welfare issues: "I speak on behalf of a large number of people outside this place … They have fears, and everyone who lives in this country believes that we are now close to the maximum number of people we can sustain in employment and underpin with our social security system" (ibid.:299). Sir John Wheeler (C), whilst welcoming cooperation on home affairs issues, asks, "Why sacrifice the advantages of being an island in the interests of a piece of Euro-dogma?" (ibid.), Finally, Quentin Davies (C) recognises a potential conundrum in arguing that "we must find a way to reconcile these two desirable and important principles—the prevention of uncontrolled immigration and the free movement of persons" (ibid.:455). Here, we can see language similar to that of the Prime Minister: references to migration being "destabilising" and "the advantages of being an island." Rumbold's anti-immigration rhetoric shows her claiming "fears" on behalf of her constituents and that the UK cannot cope with many more immigrants. On the Labour side, Peter Shore employs similar language, worrying that "What is all this about a Europe without frontiers, except to demolish the whole idea of a nation state having sovereignty and control over its own frontiers?" (ibid.:284). The *Daily Mail* follows these anti-immigration points as follows:

> The understanding all along has been that such free movement is limited by overriding national concerns about allowing in terrorists, criminals, drugs, illegal immigrants and rabies. The commission argues that, with the common frontier in place, there can be no excuse for any kind of internal restrictions. Britain says the common frontier is full of leaks. Some member countries in southern Europe simply cannot stop the influx from Africa. Germany cannot limit entry to asylum-seekers because that right is part of its constitution.
>
> In these circumstances EC external border controls are virtually no controls at all. Britain will certainly fight their removal. Indeed it is inconceivable that the Government would allow such a politically sensitive matter as control of immigration to pass out of its hands while present conditions persist. (Daily Mail 1992b)

Once again, linkages are clearly drawn between immigration and security issues like terrorism, criminality, and drugs (not to mention rabies). Overall, this minor theme contains very clear definitions of self and other, with a migrant other linked to a range of serious security concerns, thereby endangering the island self. Whilst some anti-immigration concerns here are focused on those from outside the European Community, Quentin Davies recognises the problem that freedom of movement creates for those worried about immigration. These debates about immigration are clearly linked to those on sovereignty. This makes sense if we consider sovereignty as the slash between self/other, with prospective immigrants seeking to transition across the slash as represented by the English Channel.

4.5   The Social Protocol

The debates on the merits of the Social Protocol (also referred to as "the social chapter" despite not being a formal chapter of the Maastricht Treaty) form a second minor theme in the discourse. Although I have categorised the theme as minor, it should be noted that it occupies more place than the previous immigration theme. The debate about the Social Protocol splits cleanly down left/right lines. The Prime Minister describes the protocol as "a triumph of ideology over common sense," arguing that "signing the social chapter would have removed from employers and employees in this country their right to determine for themselves such matters as working conditions" (Hansard 1992–1993a:208 col.269). This view is supported by his fellow party members, with Stephen Milligan (C) noting that "The decision to opt out of the social chapter is not only right but sets a useful precedent for negotiations with the new countries that will come in from eastern Europe" (ibid.:325). George Gardiner (C) brings federalism into his critique of the Social Protocol, arguing that "the federalists wanted us to be bound by the social chapter, which would have allowed majority voting to determine our industrial relations law and other related matters" (ibid.:368). Hugh Dykes (C) employs intertextuality in mentioning a Confederation of British Industry campaign. This enables Dykes to build authority through reference to a respected business organisation:

> We have seen the campaign launched by the CBI saying that we did not want to be hamstrung or handicapped by some social charter provisions that would strike adversely at Britain's growing economic and commercial recovery which has resulted in the past few years from successful economic management by a Conservative Government who are now in their fourth term. (ibid.:338)

The Times welcomes the fact that that "Britain alone has avoided the expense and constraints of the social chapter" (The Times 1992a).

The Labour leader Neil Kinnock, unsurprisingly, disagrees strongly: "the Government's social chapter opt-out is not only an injustice against the British people, but also contradicts Britain's economic interests" (Hansard 1992–1993a:208 col.276). Kinnock's party supports his line. Clive Betts (L) argues that "it is a disgrace that the Government should have opted out of the social chapter. That is a denial of the rights of employees in this country and undermines equality" (ibid.:412). Greg Pope (L) asks, "When will the Government learn that exploitation damages not only our economy but the fabric of our society, whereas decent pay and conditions benefit the economy and society?" (ibid.:323). John Smith, who ascended to the leadership of the Labour Party during the ratification debates, asserts that:

> [T]he Government have no ambition for the social progress that the rest of the Community seeks and which is embodied in the protocol attached to the Maastricht Treaty. We regret very much that Britain is excluded from that and from the decision taking process in the years ahead. The Government have shown no real understanding of the economic challenges of the decade

ahead. Both those tendencies are present in their opposition to the social chapter and in their opt-out mentality. (ibid.:585)

The debates at the end of the ratification process, on 22 and 23 July 1993, were ostensibly about the Social Protocol. These debates involved arguments similar to those mentioned earlier, though with the additional layer that defeat during these debates would likely lead to the dissolution of Parliament and a general election.

4.6   PORTRAYALS OF PARTY DIVISION

The defining aspect of John Major's premiership was his party's internecine warfare over Europe, so, once again, party divisions form an important element of the discourse. Near the outset of the Maastricht debates, the *Daily Mail* worries that "Barely two months after the relief of winning a small Commons majority, members of the Government are flirting with factionalism. If Mr Major is to shape a Europe nearer to Britain's desire, then he must ensure that his Cabinet keeps both its confidences and its cool" (Daily Mail 1992a). Major's attempts to achieve this are heavily criticised. John Taylor (UUP) claims that "The Government's policy … has been determined in order to hold the support of most Conservative Back Benchers and also, I fear, to deceive our Community allies in the other 11 countries who now significantly misunderstand the United Kingdom's attitude to the European Community" (Hansard 1992–1993a:208 col. 329). Giles Radice (L) agrees, noting that:

[T]he problem that the Bill presents for the Opposition is that parts of it were designed specifically to appease the Thatcherites, and in particular the two opt-outs negotiated at Maastricht. The right to opt out of European monetary union was patently a device to buy Mrs. Thatcher's support and that of a number of Thatcherite Members. (ibid.:544)

The rebellions by Conservative backbenchers during the passage of the Bill demonstrate that these attempts were less than successful. As the *Daily Mail* notes just before the final debates, division over Europe "has done more than anything else to curdle the authority of this Government and of the Prime Minister" (Daily Mail 1993). A similar line in *The Times*, asserts that "The prime minister is risking his career, the future accomplishments of his administration and his responsibility to lead Europe into a new co-operative order" (The Times 1992c). John Smith, speaking on the final day of the ratification debates, affirms that the Prime Minister "has been backed against the wall and forced, in order to survive, to threaten his own party with electoral suicide" (Hansard 1992–1993b:229 col. 633). Paddy Ashdown takes a similar line, noting that "the Prime Minister's strategy has totally failed. The Prime Minister has failed to provide a lead to his party and to the country. He has been more concerned to behave towards his party as a Government Whip than towards his nation as its Prime Minister and leader. That has been the Prime Minister's fatal mistake" (ibid.:644).

The obvious change from 1975 is the shift in focus from Labour to Conservative divisions. The aforementioned representations show that the Labour Party of 1992–1993 was far from united over Europe, but freed from the responsibility of government, these divisions were easier to manage than John Major's chronic problems with leading a riven Conservative Party.

4.7   CHAPTER CONCLUSION

In overall terms, the discourse on Europe analysed here is more interlinked and complex than in it was in 1975, in that Eurosceptics in particular seek to mutually strengthen their arguments across the three major themes. Arguments about one issue are developed in terms of another, such as Eurosceptics framing EMU as a prospective loss of sovereignty through ceding control of economic policy to Europe. Rather than breaking down into purely pro-/anti-Market camps like in 1975, a third position was identifiable in the Maastricht debates, voiced by Government figures trying to obtain ratification of the treaty whilst affecting an air of qualified scepticism. Even with this third position, it is the outright Eurosceptics like William Cash who hold the strongest place in the discourse. I would also observe that Sovereignty and Democracy has a greater degree of importance in the discourse than Centralisation, Federalisation, and Subsidiarity or EMU, although not by much. Clear definitions of self and other are present, with repeated representation of an island self at threat from an anti-democratic other based in Europe. The sceptical voices on the Conservative side have, over the two decades since the referendum, increased in number and volume to outnumber the Labour sceptics. Similar voices on the Labour side are still present, but it is fair to say that the rather mildewed metaphor of a pendulum swinging is hard to resist when considering this particular change in the discourse.

Notes

1. European issues have been debated and voted on multiple times, whether it is through multiple referenda on the same subject in Ireland and Denmark or these two debates on the Social Protocol.
2. Once again, I produced a Word document containing all the relevant material to enable straightforward reading, analysis, and searching.
3. Subsidiarity is explained by the European Union as follows: "The purpose of the subsidiarity principle is to ensure that decisions are taken at the closest possible level to citizens, by verifying that there is a clear benefit in taking the action at Union level rather than at national, regional or local level. Specifically, it is the principle whereby the Union does not take action (except in the areas which fall within its exclusive competence) unless it is more effective than action taken at national, regional or local level" (European Union Committee of the Regions. n.d.).
4. The European Commission, European Central Bank, and International Monetary Fund.

References

Ash, T. G. (2001). Is Britain European? *International Affairs, 77*(1), 1–14.

Baker, D. (2002). Elite discourse and popular opinion on European Union. British exceptionalism revisited. *Politique européenne, 6*(2), 18–35.

Baker, D., Gamble, A., & Ludlam, S. (1994). The Parliamentary siege of Maastricht 1993: Conservative divisions and British ratification. *Parliamentary Affairs, 47*(1), 37–60.

Booker, C., & North, R. (2005). *The great deception: Can the European Union survive?* (2nd ed). London: Continuum. xii, 643 p. pp.

Daily Mail. (1992a, May 8). Free entry to Britain by order. *Daily Mail.*

Daily Mail. (1992b, December 14). Roll out the pork barrel. *Daily Mail.*

Daily Mail. (1992c, April 30). Why Europe is not what it was. *Daily Mail.*

Daily Mail. (1992d, November 4). Why the Tories must back John Major. *Daily Mail.*

Daily Mail. (1993, May 17). The Danes do it their way. *Daily Mail.*

Delanty, G. (2008). Fear of others: Social exclusion and the European crisis of solidarity. *Social Policy & Administration, 42*(6), 676–690.

European Union Committee of the Regions. (n.d.). *Subsidiarity and proportionality—essential principles.* Subsidiarity: From Maastricht to Lisbon. Retrieved

March 5, from https://portal.cor.europa.eu/subsidiarity/whatis/Pages/SubsidiarityfromMaastrichttoLisbon.aspx. .

Fontana, C., & Parsons, C. (2015). 'One Woman's Prejudice': Did Margaret Thatcher cause Britain's anti-Europeanism? *JCMS: Journal of Common Market Studies, 53*(1), 89–105.

Foucault, M. (2004). *Society must be defended: Lectures at the College de France, 1975–1976.* London: Penguin. xxiii, 310 p. pp.

Hansard. (1992-3a). House of Commons Debates. Vol. 208, Col. 261–470, 509–600

Hansard. (1992-3b). House of Commons Debates. Vol. 229, Col. 625–724

Harmsen, R., & Spiering, M. (2004). *Euroscepticism: Party politics, national identity and European integration.* European studies. Amsterdam: Rodopi. 290 p. pp.

Huysmans, J. (2000). The European Union and the securitization of migration. *JCMS: Journal of Common Market Studies, 38*(5), 751–777.

Kettle, M. (2005, 4 April). Pollsters taxed. *The Guardian.*

Pollack, M. A. (2000). The end of creeping competence? EU policy-making since maastricht. *JCMS: Journal of Common Market Studies, 38*(3), 519–538.

The Times. (1992a, November 4). Empty Threats. *The Times.*

The Times. (1992b, September 14). Free the Pound. *The Times.*

The Times. (1992c, September 16). Politics before pride. *The Times.*

The Times. (1992d, 26 September). Pushing by Bonn. *The Times.*

The Times. (1993a, April 13). Federalist fault lines. *The Times.*

The Times. (1993b, May 17). Voting for Europe. *The Times.*

Young, H. (1998). *This blessed plot: Britain and Europe from Churchill to Blair.* London: Macmillan. xiv, 558, 24 p. of plates pp.

CHAPTER 5

The British Discourse on Europe 2013: Cameron and the Second Referendum

Abstract This chapter analyses the proto-referendum debates of 2013, beginning with David Cameron's Bloomberg speech. This speech set out the Prime Minister's intention to renegotiate the UK's relationship with the EU and commitment to hold an in/out referendum on EU membership. The major themes in the discourse are identified as *Sovereignty and Democracy*, *Immigration*; and *Economy, Jobs, and Prosperity*. The chapter observes that Pro-European voices occupy a minor position in the discourse of 2013. It is Eurosceptics of both the more qualified, "soft" variety like the Prime Minister and the outright rejectionist, "hard" Eurosceptics like UKIP leader Nigel Farage who predominate. An important change in the discourse is that immigration has become a major part of the debate since 1992–1993.

Keywords Referendum • Immigration • Sovereignty • Democracy • Economy • Eurozone crisis

This chapter analyses the debates of 2013 about the UK's membership of the EU. These debates began in earnest when, on 23 January, the Prime Minister made a major speech in which he announced his intention to renegotiate the UK's relationship with the EU and, should the Conservative Party win the general election in 2015, hold an in/out referendum on membership by 2017. With regard to my research questions, this chapter

© The Editor(s) (if applicable) and The Author(s) 2016
J. Todd, *The UK's Relationship with Europe*,
DOI 10.1007/978-3-319-33669-5_5

provides the third part of the picture in assessing the patterns in the British discourse on Europe. With this being the third and most recent period under analysis, it will also be possible to draw out the major *changes* and significant *continuities* across the 40 years that encompass these three discursive peaks. As mentioned later in the text, the issue of immigration is a major theme in the discourse here, and thus is addressed in some detail. The *implications* will be drawn out in more detail in the final chapter. The discourse analysed here can be seen as a "proto-referendum debate" and covers January–December 2013.

Following the formation of the Conservative–Liberal Democrat coalition government in 2010, the debate on the UK's membership of the EU became increasingly intense. Conservative backbenchers, many unhappy with the compromises that are a feature of life in a coalition, became increasingly restive through 2011 and 2012 (see, for example Cowley and Stuart 2012). The Prime Minister came under sustained pressure from these backbench MPs to commit to a referendum on Europe (they had previously been angered by Cameron's decision against holding a referendum on the Treaty of Lisbon). This pressure coincided with the continued rise of the UKIP under the flamboyant leadership of Nigel Farage (see Tournier-Sol 2015a). More than 100 Conservative MPs signed a letter to the Prime Minster in summer 2012, urging him to hold a referendum on Europe (see Montgomerie 2012). The Prime Minister however argued in a newspaper op-ed column that "I don't agree with those who say we should leave and therefore want the earliest possible in/out referendum" (Cameron 2012).

However, this pressure was sustained through the autumn; in January 2013, the Prime Minister made a major speech in which he announced his intention to renegotiate the UK's relationship with the EU and, should the Conservatives win the next general election, hold an in/out referendum on the UK's continued membership of the EU (Cameron 2013). For an overview of the run-up to, delivery of and reception to the speech, see Daddow (2015b) and Seldon and Snowdon (2015). This announcement failed to appease the Eurosceptic wing of the Conservative Party, with 114 MPs voting on an amendment to the Queen's speech (the speech that sets out the government's legislative programme for the Parliamentary session ahead). This amendment expressed regret about the absence of a bill making provision for an in/out referendum (see Wintour and Watt 2013). Following this highly unusual step, the Private Member's Bill on an in/out referendum was introduced by the Conservative backbencher

James Wharton. His Bill received the support of the Conservative Party and the studied indifference of Labour and the Liberal Democrats during its passage through the Commons. The Bill was not introduced by the government because the Liberal Democrats (then in coalition with the larger Conservative Party) did not agree with David Cameron's referendum commitment. Instead, a Conservative backbencher introduced the legislation as a Private Member's Bill.[1] The Bill completed its passage through the House of Commons on 29 November 2013, but failed to make it through the House of Lords.

Two other brief pieces of context to highlight are as follows. First, at the start of 2014, the UK's restrictions on freedom of movement from Bulgaria and Romania came to an end. This has relevance for the immigration debates. Second, the crisis in the Eurozone was of course in full swing through much of 2013; this played into the debates on the economic implications of EU membership (see Macmillan 2015).

The discourse analysed here includes the following:

- Prime Minister David Cameron's speech at Bloomberg on 23 January. This speech set the terms for the debate over the rest of the year.
- Parliamentary debates on the European Union (Referendum) Bill 2013. This Bill would have stipulated that a referendum on the UK's membership of the EU must be held before the end of 2017. Whilst a Private Member's Bill, the debate included contributions from the then Foreign Secretary William Hague and the then Shadow Foreign Secretary Douglas Alexander. The debates analysed are the second and third readings of the Bill and amount to 50,000 words.[2]
- Nigel Farage's party conference speech from 20 September 2013. As leader of the hard Eurosceptic United Kingdom Independence Party (UKIP), Farage holds an important position in the discourse on Europe. His party conference speech sets out the UKIP position on Europe and reflects his contributions to the discourse throughout the year.
- Newspaper editorials from *The Times*, the *Daily Mail*, the *Daily Mirror*, and *The Sun*. More than 100 editorials addressing the referendum and/or European issues were analysed.

Like during the Maastricht debates, there are three overall positions to observe: hard Eurosceptics (e.g. Nigel Farage), soft Eurosceptics (e.g.

David Cameron) and pro-Europeans. David Cameron's speech frames the discourse and takes in a number of important themes, including two major themes I term *Sovereignty and Democracy*; and *Economy, Jobs, and Prosperity* (Cameron makes much of these issues in his speech), and two minor themes I label as *EU Reform*; and *Trusting the People*. The remaining major theme was *Immigration*, which features in the Parliamentary debates and, in particular, in the newspaper editorials and Nigel Farage's speech. As in previous chapters, a brief analysis of *Portrayals of Party Divisions* is described before the chapter concludes.

As before, the party affiliations of backbench MPs are set out as follows: L—Labour, C—Conservative, LD—Liberal Democrat, and DUP—Democratic Unionist Party. Where appropriate, I group quotes from similar sources (e.g. Labour pro-Europeans).

5.1   Sovereignty and Democracy

The first theme, Sovereignty and Democracy, has been a major issue in all three of the periods analysed. This theme is dominated by those who proclaim dissatisfaction with what they see as negative consequences of EU membership for the UK's sovereignty and democracy. David Cameron is an important voice here, addressing issues of sovereignty and democracy, in detail, during his speech. He makes an explicit link between identity and foreign policy as follows:

> I know that the United Kingdom is sometimes seen as an argumentative and rather strong-minded member of the family of European nations. And it's true that our geography has shaped our psychology. We have the character of an island nation—independent, forthright, passionate in defence of our sovereignty. We can no more change this British sensibility than we can drain the English Channel. And because of this sensibility, we come to the European Union with a frame of mind that is more practical than emotional. For us, the European Union is a means to an end—prosperity, stability, the anchor of freedom and democracy both within Europe and beyond her shores—not an end in itself. (Cameron 2013)

Cameron goes on to note that "there is a gap between the EU and its citizens which has grown dramatically in recent years. And which represents a lack of democratic accountability and consent that is—yes—felt particularly acutely in Britain" (ibid). He similarly affirms that "there is a growing frustration that the EU is seen as something that is done to people rather than acting on their behalf" and that "democratic consent for the EU in Britain is now wafer thin" (ibid). Vail (2015:118) describes this as Cameron "criticiz[ing] the EU as an existential threat to Britain's national sovereignty." The Prime Minister concludes that "we need to have a bigger and more significant role for national parliaments. *There is not, in my view, a single European demos.* It is national parliaments, which are, and will remain, the true source of real democratic legitimacy and accountability in the EU" (ibid, emphasis added). These excerpts from the speech show the Prime Minister advocating British exceptionalism through reference to an "independent" and "forthright" country that is an "island nation." This reference to an "island nation" is a form of intertextuality, in that it is a programmatic catchphrase. As mentioned previously, this particular catchphrase brings to mind Churchillian wartime speeches. Daddow (2015a:80) has noted that Thatcher, Blair, and Cameron have all made reference to the "island" status and its use in justifying the UK's exceptional position with regard to European integration.

The Prime Minister rejects the notion of a "single European demos" (i.e. a single European self) and prioritises national parliaments, thereby privileging the national "self" and rejecting a shared sense of European identity. Indeed, I view this as a very clear demonstration of Neumann's (1999:35) assertion that "delineation of self and other is an active and ongoing part of identity formation." As Marcussen et al. (1999:628) observe: "classical *Anglo-Saxon* notions of political order emphasize parliamentary democracy and external sovereignty. ... Thus, there is not much space for 'Europe' or 'Europeanness' in this particular British political discourse." More broadly, de Wilde et al. (2014:766) also observe that democracy is a "primary concern in EU polity contestation."

Conservative backbenchers take these arguments further, often arguing for a defence of British sovereignty through reference to history, and especially to the Second World War. Richard Shepherd (C) assets that:

"This vote, what we decide and what people in the future decide will determine the character and strength of our national constitutional history, which is being threatened. Why should we defer in such an adventure, when this is the most remarkable and ancient of all the democratic communities within western Europe? Why?" (Hansard 2013–2014a:565 col. 1201–2)

William Cash (C) uses the highest form of nominal intertextuality possible in the UK by appealing to Churchill. He states, "People have fought and died. The only reason we live in the United Kingdom in peace and prosperity is because, in the second and first world wars, we stood up for that freedom and democracy. Churchill galvanised the British people to stand up for the very principles that are now at stake" (ibid:1210). Like in the previous chapters, the Second World War is an essential reference point for those debating European issues. As Daddow (2006:320) notes:

> This is the kind of commonsense history everyone knows even if they are not historians ... the kind that tells us all we need to know about Europe from Britain's martial past; its encounters with the Spanish Armada, at the battle of Trafalgar, with Napoleon at Waterloo, after the let-down of Munich in 1938 and against Hitler's Germany during the Second World War.

Hawkins (2012:568) too states that the EU is "seen to pose the same danger to British freedom and democracy as Nazi Germany. The UK is linked to democratic ideals through being described as "the most ancient and remarkable of democratic communities". The framing of continental Europe as a threat is clear in the quotations above, with "our national constitutional history ... being threatened" and that at stake are the principles of freedom and democracy for which "Churchill galvanised the British people to stand up."

Despite their political differences, Nigel Farage uses notably similar imagery and identity-based arguments to the Prime Minister in building his hard Eurosceptic case. Like Cameron, Farage asserts that the UK is different because of its geography:

> [T]he fact is we just don't belong in the European Union. Britain is different. Our geography puts us apart. Our history puts us apart. Our institutions produced by that history put us apart. We think differently. We behave differently. ... The roots go back seven, eight, nine hundred years with the Common Law. Civil rights. Habeas corpus. The presumption of innocence. The right to a trial by jury. On the continent confession is the mother of all evidence. (Farage 2013)

This is a clear example of othering, with Farage appealing to the weight of "seven, eight, nine hundred years" of history, in which "Britain is different." Farage uses ethical dimensions of identity to differentiate between a British tradition of presumption of innocence and jury trial from a continental system based on confession. Tournier-Sol (2015b:142) has observed UKIP's focus both on the theme of democracy, describing it as "a central element of UKIP's thinking," and on defending national sovereignty. Indeed, Farage also states that "We know that only by leaving the union can we regain control of our borders, our parliament, democracy and our ability to trade freely with the fastest-growing economies in the world" (Farage 2013). Here, we can see a link to the two other major themes in the discourse: immigration and the economy. Like with the excerpt from David Cameron's speech earlier in the text, Farage here substantiates Neumann (1999:140) in employing cultural differentiation to serve his political cause of achieving a British exit from Europe.

A number of Labour MPs are also concerned about issues of sovereignty and democracy. Ian Davidson (L), with an amusing bit of pop-culture-inspired intertextuality, argues that the UK's position should be "that the inexorable expansion of the EU's powers—like the Blob in the science fiction films that used to replicate itself every 24 hours and expand into new areas—is halted and constrained" (Hansard 2013–2014a:565 col. 1205). Graham Stringer (L) is concerned that "This House, by signing various treaties, has taken away from the British people the right to throw out the rascals who are making their laws" (ibid:1229). Nigel Dodds (DUP) agrees, arguing that "Over the past three decades, there has been a steady transfer of powers from our sovereign Parliament here at Westminster to the corridors and back alleys of Brussels—a process that still continues on a weekly and monthly basis, inexorably and inevitably, in the pursuit of the goal of ever-closer political union" (ibid:1215). Once again, aspersions are cast against the city of Brussels, its bureaucracy, and its apparently treacherous back alleys to create a sense of threat from Europe.

These concerns about sovereignty and democracy are echoed by both *The Times* and the *Daily Mail*. An editorial from *The Times* argues that "a union worth preserving would be one that valued national sovereignty, not only for this nation but for any that wished it, and which was willing to reform to advance the prosperity of its members" (The Times 2013e), The *Daily Mail* is more strongly critical:

> According to José Manuel Barroso, any country that wishes to re-claim powers from Brussels risks taking Europe back to the 'divisions' that led to the First World War. Doubtless, the unelected president of the EU Commission

is worried that, if the voters of Britain are given a say over our future membership by David Cameron, the verdict may not be to his liking. So, with typical contempt for democracy, he raises the spectre of the 'trenches' to try to intimidate us back into line. Yet it is Mr Barroso's claim that the EU has brought 'peace' to Europe that is most risible. For the painful reality is that, by imposing the hopelessly-flawed single currency on its citizens, the EU has sparked terrifying social and economic unrest across great swathes of the continent. (Daily Mail 2013b)

The *Daily Mail* editorial includes a classic Eurosceptic trope: reference to an "unelected" European figure and, importantly, the assertion of this figure's "contempt for democracy." The *Daily Mail* is using ethical dimensions of identity here to differentiate between an anti-democratic EU and the UK.

One of the few arguments from a pro-European perspective was from Martin Horwood (LD). He argues via explicit intertextuality that one of the alternative models favoured by Eurosceptics would have unfavourable democratic implications:

This morning, The Daily Telegraph, I think, quoted the leader of the Norwegian Conservative party, who pointed out that the supposed solution of the UK trying to have a status more or less equivalent to Norway's was worse than being in the EU. Norway pays hundreds of billions of euros to the European Union for access to the single European market, and finds out about the rules through so-called fax democracy. (Hansard 2013–2014a:565 col. 1228)

In summarising this theme, I note that the Eurosceptic representation of sovereignty and democracy under threat (whether of the "soft" variety like the Prime Minister or "hard" like Nigel Farage) are strongly dominant in the discourse. Their arguments, drawing once more on a history of threat from continental Europe and a self-proclaimed island identity, call for a transfer of sovereignty back from the EU to the UK. In some cases (e.g. Nigel Farage, William Cash) this call is for a total transfer back and in others (David Cameron in particular) the call is more qualified. The discourse here shows a strong degree of continuity from the previous two periods. The EU is again represented as anti-democratic and as a threat to the sovereignty of the British parliament and the independence of the UK as a nation state.

5.2 Immigration

The second major theme in the 2013 discourse is the issue of immigration. Fears about immigration feature more heavily in the editorials than in the Parliamentary discourse, though a number of backbenchers mention it. Those who do bring up the issue in connection with the debate on Europe generally do so from a negative perspective. *The Times*, the *Daily Mail*, and *The Sun* all devote a considerable number of editorial column inches to problematizing immigration, whilst in his party conference speech, Nigel Farage describes immigration as "the biggest single issue facing this country" (Farage 2013). During the period under analysis here the focus was almost exclusively on intra-EU migration: the subsequent refugee crisis has recently become an additional element in the discourse.

In the Parliamentary debate, Andrew Percy (C) makes reference to the impact of "uncontrolled EU immigration" (Hansard 2013–2014a:565 col. 1177), whilst Priti Patel (C) argues that immigration rules "have been imposed on us. We have not had a say" (ibid:1236). Nigel Dodds (DUP) combines these two perspectives, asking "How many times do we hear complaints about untrammelled immigration from EU countries as we no longer have the power effectively to control our own borders?" (ibid:1215). This issue of control is also brought up by Adam Afriyie (C), who asserts that "people want to know that their Government are already fighting to get control of our borders" (ibid:1238). These concerns are not limited to those on the right of the political spectrum. For example, Ian Davidson (L) states that "We have to have control over our borders, which means saying to our European colleagues that we do not accept unfettered free movement of people if it is not in the United Kingdom's interest at any particular given time" (ibid:1205). The representation of loss of control is consistent through the immigration references in the Parliamentary debate. *The Times*, although the least negative of the three right-leaning newspapers when it comes to immigration, also develops the representation of loss of control in a 23 November editorial:

> As the country prepares for a fresh influx of migrant workers from Romania and Bulgaria, their impact may or not may not become a serious social challenge. ... In a new Times poll of attitudes on Europe and immigration, anxieties that Britain lacks control over its borders are the overwhelming concern of voters asked what Mr Cameron should focus on when renegotiating the European relationship...

> Our poll shows that voters of all political persuasions are far more con-
> cerned about the impact of new immigration on housing and public services
> than on crime, inter-ethnic relations or even the availability of jobs. (The
> Times 2013c)

The following two quotes demonstrate another aspect of the immigration discourse, namely, the employment of "welfare chauvinism." The
term welfare chauvinism was coined by Anderson and Bjørklund (1990)
and describes the perspective that state support like unemployment benefit should be restricted to national citizens and not provided to those
"others" originating elsewhere:

> **The Times:** If the European Commission wanted to give succour to
> Nigel Farage, it could hardly have done better than attack Britain's tests
> for European Union migrants who claim welfare benefits. The commission
> claims its aim is equality: that Britain's "right to reside" test discriminates
> against non-British EU citizens because British citizens do not have to pass
> it. In fact, this is a blatant attempt to use freedom of movement to open a
> new front in the war to restrict the power of nation states in matters of deep
> national significance. (The Times 2013c)
>
> **The Sun:** Ministers continue to duck questions about the scale of a new
> wave of immigration from Eastern Europe. So Migration Watch, a respected
> independent campaign group, has worked it out for them. The organisation
> estimates that up to 350,000 from Bulgaria, the EU's poorest country, and
> Romania will arrive over the next five years. Under EU rules, we are power-
> less to deny them entry or benefits once restrictions are lifted next January.
> (The Sun 2013a)

A *Daily Mail* editorial similarly complains of "yet another sovereignty-
sapping power grab" from an "EU elite," which is "trying to seize control not only of Britain's borders, but also our welfare state" (Daily Mail
2013a). These excerpts align with Huysmans' view that "For welfare
chauvinists, immigrants and asylum-seekers are not simply rivals but illegitimate claimants of socio-economic rights" (2000:767). The editorials
here clearly use spatial dimensions of identity, with *The Sun* raising the
prospect of 350,000 impoverished migrants arriving from Romania and
Bulgaria over the coming five years. These arrivals and their countries of
origin are linked by *The Sun* to a set of EU rules that prevent the UK
from denying them either entry or benefits. In the following quote, the

Daily Mail makes explicit reference to a threat to national identity from immigration:

> For well over a decade, opinion polls have shown substantial majorities in favour of cutting immigration to a rate at which it can be comfortably absorbed. Yet in this supposed democracy, politicians have simply ignored those who elected them. Indeed, less than eight weeks from today, under orders from the EU, the Coalition plans to throw open our borders to any of 29 million Bulgarians and Romanians who choose to settle here. With our national identity at stake, the time to start listening is now. The first step must surely be to defy Brussels and declare that the UK is full up. (Daily Mail 2013c)

These editorials clearly employ a discourse of fear, with repeated reference to loss of control, powerlessness, and waves of immigration culminating in a *Daily Mail* claim that "our national identity is at stake." This fits with Spiering's (2002:69–70) observation that Eurosceptics "claim that the European Union threatens the viability and future of existing national identities." Huysmans (2000:769) too describes the use of metaphors that present immigrants "as a serious threat to the survival of the socio-economic system." The theme of fear is also employed when linking immigration to crime. Nigel Farage alleges that "London is already experiencing a Romanian crime wave. There have been an astounding 27,500 arrests in the Metropolitan Police area in the last five years. 92 per cent of ATM crime is committed by Romanians" (Farage 2013). He then concludes that "This gets to the heart of the immigration policy that UKIP wants, we should not welcome foreign criminal gangs and we must deport those who have committed offences" (ibid.). An editorial in *The Sun* takes a similar view:

> Today The Sun reveals the shocking figure that nearly one in five of all rape or murder suspects is foreign. The sheer scale of crimes committed by foreigners is astonishing. Confront politicians with an embarrassing statistic and they try to get off the hook by talking about "context". So here's some context for that crime figure. A report published today shows that, because of a loophole in the immigration rules, more than 20,000 foreigners from outside the EU come to live here every year. It doesn't take a genius to work out that the two figures might be connected. The more foreigners who live here, the more likely it is that crimes will be committed by foreigners. The Government is trying to get a grip on immigration. The numbers overall are

down. But crime figures like this show just how vital it is that loopholes are closed and sanity is restored to immigration. (The Sun 2013d)

These references combine what Buonfino (2004) describes as the social and economic threats of migration. The previous two quotes are clearly attempts to frame immigration and, by extension, the EU itself as a threat by associating those arriving in the UK with criminality. Nigel Farage repeatedly labels Romanian people as criminals in his contributions to the discourse on Europe. Balzacq (2012:69) notes that such stereotyping forms part of a process of securitisation. References of threat from waves of immigration to the British national identity are another element of this securitising move. The discourse also presents economic threats in terms of pressure on housing and public services. The presence of these threats supports Huysmans' (2000:752) conclusion that "migration has been increasingly presented as a threat to public order, cultural identity, and domestic labour market stability: it has been securitised."

In the interests of balance, it should be noted that, whilst the vast majority of *Sun* editorials that feature immigration are highly negative, one does strike a more positive note: "Many Poles come here to strive and prosper and contribute, not beg benefits. If such valuable migrants choose us ahead of the rest of Europe, doesn't that say good things about our country?" (The Sun 2013d). An editorial in *The Times* also takes a more nuanced stance, stating that:

Although there are undoubtedly cases of migrants coming to the UK to take up welfare entitlements, and the pressure on public services can be severe, there is not much evidence to substantiate the claim that lots of migrants are attracted to Britain because of its generous welfare state. It is much more common that people come to Britain because it pays, by southern European standards, relatively high wages." (The Times 2013a).

Finally, an editorial in the *Daily Mirror* is critical of anti-immigrant rhetoric, arguing that

David Cameron's scaremongering about so-called benefit tourists from the European Union shows the UKIP tail is wagging the Conservative dog. The Prime Minister's shameless tub-thumping is motivated by base politics, not hard facts. His sudden conversion to the anti-immigration cause reeks of Tory fear. (Daily Mirror 2013d)

Overall, this theme shows the predominance of Eurosceptics expressing anti-immigration views. They seek to frame the immigration issue as both a threat to British national identity and as intrinsically linked to the UK's membership of the EU. This representation includes strong delineation of the British self from an other that is both external (prospective migrants from Romania and Bulgaria in particular) and internal (criminal immigrant gangs and undeserving welfare recipients). This other is differentiated spatially as coming from Eastern Europe, and ethically as being responsible for crimes such as murder, rape, and ATM theft, thereby securitising migration and, by extension, EU membership. Tapping into such fears of threat to the individual self in order to create a more general sense of threat originating from Europe is a regrettably effective strategy for Eurosceptics. As Tournier-Sol (2015a:location 3007) has observed, immigration has higher salience among voters than Europe, so connecting the two issues is, from their perspective, clever. This fear-based discourse and its implications for both the UK's relationship with Europe will be addressed in more detail in the following chapter.

5.3 Economy, Jobs, and Prosperity

A third major theme in the 2013 discourse, like in the two previous chapters, addresses economic issues. As mentioned earlier, there are three positions in the discourse here. First is a position that recognises the benefits of the single market but states the need for reform and reduced regulation. Second is that of hard Eurosceptics who are highly critical of the effect of EU membership on the UK economy. Third is a position arguing against a referendum on the grounds that the prospect of a vote on EU membership creates uncertainty for business.

David Cameron is the main voice of the first position. He argues that "Continued access to the Single Market is vital for British businesses and British jobs. Since 2004, Britain has been the destination for one in five of all inward investments into Europe. And being part of the Single Market has been key to that success" (Cameron 2013). However, the Prime Minister also foresees problems ahead: "Taken as a whole, Europe's share of world output is projected to fall by almost a third in the next two decades. This is the competitiveness challenge—and much of our weakness in meeting it is self-inflicted. Complex rules restricting our labour markets are not some naturally occurring phenomenon. Just as excessive regulation is not some external plague that's been visited on our businesses" (ibid). So, whilst praising the single market as "vital" for the UK, Cameron is also critical of "complex rules restricting labour" and "excessive regulation." Like John Major before him, Cameron frames his diagnosis of Europe's economic challenges in free-market orthodoxy.

This issue of regulation is picked up by his more strongly Eurosceptic party colleagues. David Rutley (C) argues that "there are not just political reasons, but clear-cut economic reasons why we need to have a referendum, not least of which are the fact that 70% of the regulations that are an unacceptable burden on our businesses and their employees emanate from Europe" (Hansard 2013–2014a:565 col. 1210). Priti Patel (C) similarly states that "For far too long, our taxpayers have been pillaged and hard-pressed families and businesses across the country have been subjected to far too much regulation and red tape by the European Union" (ibid:1236). Patel uses another metaphor of external threat, with taxpayers apparently being "pillaged" by the EU. William Cash (C) takes a different approach, discussing the issue in terms of trade deficit (echoing his anti-Marketeer predecessors):

> With respect to our trade deficit, as I have said on a number of occasions, in 2012, according to the Office for National Statistics, had a trade deficit of £70 billion with the other 27 member states. To give the point some substance, Germany, on the other hand—no wonder there are two Europes, which are increasingly becoming German-oriented—had a trade surplus with the other 27 member states in 2011 that has now gone up to £72 billion. (ibid:1211)

David Nuttall (C) supports this, asserting "I want us to trade with our European neighbours, but I do not see why we should have to pay billions of pounds every year for the privilege of doing so, particularly when we buy more goods from them than they buy from us" (ibid:1218). These quotes show how those in favour of a referendum seek to frame EU membership as damaging to the British economy. Editorials in *The Sun* take a similar stance to Conservative Eurosceptics. For example, one refers to "the EU's suffocating employment red-tape and damaging human rights laws" and "taxpayers' money pouring into the pockets of idle, overpaid EU fatcats" (The Sun 2013b). Once again the EU is framed as hurting the economy, with its representatives lazy, over-remunerated "fatcats."

Eurosceptics on the Labour benches focus on employment and jobs. For example, John Mann (L) makes a link between jobs and immigration:

"A majority of my constituents appear to agree with me rather than with the Prime Minister that the problem with Europe is that there is too much labour market flexibility, and that people are coming in and taking jobs here (Hansard 2013–2014a:565 col. 1176). Graham Stringer (L) argues that "We have a gigantic trade deficit with the rest of the European Union, equivalent to a million jobs" and that "Hundreds of thousands and millions of jobs are being destroyed by the European Union. It is not helpful to our economy" (ibid:1230). An editorial in *The Times* argues that two issues are the major cause of Euroscepticism in the UK: the economic impact of the crisis and immigration. It states: "What used to be minority opposition to EU membership — about a quarter of voters were firmly against — has become mainstream in the wake of the eurozone crisis and its impact on Britain's economy and immigration from the EU's new eastern members over the past decade" (The Times 2013d).

The position of those opposed to a referendum is a veritable fountain of intertextuality, with economic arguments about uncertainty based on reference to a range of figures and organisations. Martin Horwood (LD) states that "The CBI is quoted in the Independent newspaper, *i*, this morning, and raises the problem of the uncertainty caused for British business: 'British businesses don't want to find themselves at the margins of the world's largest trading bloc operating under market rules over which they have no influence'" (Hansard 2013–2014a:565 col. 1228). Gordon Marsden (L) argues that "40 % of UK exports go to the EU tariff free, and that business leaders in this country have said that it would be dangerously destabilising if a referendum were to go ahead" (ibid: 1171). The Shadow Foreign Secretary, Douglas Alexander (L), similarly states that "the European chief executive of Ford has said: 'All countries should have their sovereignty, but don't discuss leaving a trading partner where 50pc of your exports go... That would be devastating for the UK economy'" (ibid:1186). Finally, Wayne David (L) affirms that:

> The Smiths Group of advanced technologies, the Weir Group of leading engineering businesses, easyJet, Ford and Toyota have all expressed concerns at the idea of the United Kingdom not having access to the single European market. As the Financial Times stated in January, "many" entrepreneurs "strongly support" Britain remaining part of the European Union. We would be profoundly mistaken to put at risk this country's economic wellbeing for the interests of the Conservative party. (ibid:1237–8)

The concern about uncertainty is reflected in the two *Daily Mirror* editorials on the day of and day after David Cameron's speech. One criticises the Prime Minister by stating that "By opening up this Pandora's Box, he creates years of uncertainty which could drive away investment from the UK, diminish our power within Europe and leave us estranged from our greatest trading partner" (Daily Mirror 2013e). The second argues that "investors will turn their back on Britain because of the uncertainty the Prime Minister has created. International companies will now think twice before building a new factory in the UK when they cannot be sure that we will still be a member of one of the world's largest trade blocs" (Daily Mirror 2013a). These uncertainty arguments bear a resemblance to the pro-Marketeer economic arguments from 1975 (summed up in Chap. 3 as "why risk leaving?")

In summarising this theme, I note that the discourse on the economic implications of membership display a good degree of continuity with the two previous periods. Whilst informed by a different context, representations of uncertainty/risk, excess regulation, and balance of trade perpetuate in the discourse of 2013.

5.4   EU Reform

Reform of the EU features as one of the minor themes in the discourse, with the Prime Minister devoting a section of his speech to calling for EU reform: "I want to speak to you today with urgency and frankness about the European Union and how it must change—both to deliver prosperity and to retain the support of its peoples" (Cameron 2013). Cameron goes on to set out his "vision for a new European union, fit for the twenty-first Century," based on five principles: "competitiveness," "flexibility," "returning power to Member States," "democratic accountability," and "fairness" (ibid). These principles are connected to the two major themes above of Sovereignty and Democracy and Economy, Jobs, and Prosperity. Once again, the Foreign Secretary follows the Prime Minister's lead. William Hague uses intertextuality to bolster his arguments for reform, which he links to protecting British sovereignty and democracy:

> the EU needs reform if it is to be democratically sustainable for all its members, which it will not be if ever-greater centralisation sucks ever more powers from its member states. As the Dutch Government's recent report

stated, "the time of 'ever closer union' in every possible...area is behind us". They are right. Our policy is therefore to seek reform so that the EU can be more competitive and flexible for the modern age, so that powers can come back to the countries of the European Union, and so that national Parliaments—the indispensible [sic] vessels of democracy—can have a more powerful role and then put the decision in the hands of the British people, as this Bill would do. (Hansard 2013–2014a:565 col. 1190)

An editorial in *The Sun* pithily observes that the Prime Minister "wants to slash Brussels interference and put bossy bureaucrats back in their box" (The Sun 2013c). High-profile Labour figures also agree that reform is necessary. The Shadow Foreign Secretary Douglas Alexander notes that "There is of course pressing work to be done, on which I hope there is cross-party agreement, such as the completion of the single market and its extension into digital, energy and finance" (Hansard 2013–2014a:565 col. 1187). There are some voices more sceptical about the prospects for reform. Graham Stringer (L) asks:

Do hon. Members really think that Ireland, Germany, Italy and the newer members of the EU, many of whom have to have referendums before they can take a decision on the constitution, will vote to change the treaty of Rome, or of Lisbon, Nice, Amsterdam, Maastricht, or any of the others? ... I do not believe that renegotiation is possible. (ibid:1230)

An editorial in *The Times* takes a similar view:

European politicians have failed to take advantage of the breathing space offered by calmer markets to introduce the reforms needed to put the EU on a stronger footing. The weather forecast for Europe is prolonged depression. At the same time, the EU appears determined, for no good reason, to undermine Britain, and to offer little hope that Mr Cameron's promised renegotiation will come to anything. UKIP stole the headlines with its performance in Eastleigh. But the EU is providing us with good reason to worry about what is going on in Europe. We should all be Eurosceptics now. (The Times 2013b)

This editorial represents the EU as opposed to the UK and its reform goals and urges Euroscepticism as the only viable perspective. Overall, hard Eurosceptics hold a relatively minimal position here: they are interested more in exit than in reform.

5.5   TRUSTING THE PEOPLE

The second minor theme encompasses a debate about the referendum commitment and trust of the British people. Those in favour of a referendum seek to make common cause with "the people" and take credit for trusting them with the issue of EU membership. William Hague describes the need "to give the British people their democratic right to have their say on this country's future" (Hansard 2013–2014a:565 col. 1193). William Cash (C) rounds off his speech with a flourish along similar lines:

> I conclude with a simple statement: this is about trust. It is about trust in people. Because we are doing it through a Bill, as is required, we will give authority through Parliament to have a referendum. That is what this is all about. It is to give the British people their right to have their say. (ibid:1212)

For Labour, Frank Field builds on this theme, stating that "this is a matter not just of us trusting the British voters, but of the possibility of them trusting us a little bit more in return" (ibid:1236). An editorial in *The Times* bolsters this viewpoint, arguing that "The relationship between the EU and its members has changed greatly since 1975, and the British people deserve the chance to decide if they want to be a part of what the common market that they committed to has now become" (The Times 2013e).

Other Labour figures are more critical. Chi Onwurah argues that "Democracy is about more than just voting and a referendum every 30 years or so; it is about debate and engagement too" (Hansard 2013–2014b:571 col. 572). She concludes that "My fear, therefore, is that any debate preceding a referendum, at a time when European economies are in so much trouble, will not be based on a sober reading and reporting of the facts" (ibid.). Nigel Farage also brings up the issue of trust, but from a perspective of mistrusting the Prime Minister: "So Mr. Cameron wants a referendum … well we've heard it all before with his 'cast iron guarantee' and we don't believe that he is sincere. The use of the word renegotiation is no more than a cynical tactic to kick the issue into the long grass after the next election" (Farage 2013). Here, we can see Farage using trust as a party-political issue. The link between Europe and party politics will be discussed in more detail in the following section.

This minor theme shows a change since the debates of 1975, where the constitutional significance of holding a referendum received a good degree of criticism. Such criticism from a constitutional perspective is not present in the 2013 debate: this goes to show that referenda are now part of the constitutional landscape of the UK (see also Forman 2003:314).

5.6   PORTRAYALS OF PARTY DIVISION

Party divisions about Europe have been a consistent feature of the discourse across the three periods under analysis, with the focus in 2013 to a large extent on divisions within the Conservative Party and its loss of support to UKIP. The number of Eurosceptic MPs has increased since the Maastricht debates, including the majority of the 2010 intake of Conservative MPs (Alexandre-Collier 2015; Lynch 2015). With regard to party divisions, Douglas Alexander (L) notes that "The Bill is not being debated because Conservative Back Benchers trust the public; it is being debated because Conservative Back Benchers do not trust the Prime Minister" (Hansard 2013–2014a:565 col. 1181). Gisela Stuart (L) similarly asserts that "the whole reason we need this Bill is because the Conservative Party does not trust its own Prime Minister to implement legislation after the next general election" (ibid:1232). Mike Gapes (L) states that the "This is a political ploy to try to assuage the Europhobic wing of the Tory party and to keep them on board" (Hansard (2013–2014):571 col. 583). The *Daily Mirror* follows this line of argument and argues itself in favour of continuity from the Maastricht debates: "Europe is the issue which gets obsessive Tory MPs out of bed. … Mr Cameron resembles John Major more every day and he will be devoured by an irrelevant obsession with a subject which matters little to most voters" (Daily Mirror 2013c). The editorial line of *The Times* is interesting to observe. It moves from a position of arguing that the Prime Minister's referendum commitment will provide a fillip to part unity in January to likening him to John Major in May:

> **January:** In promising an in/out referendum on European Union membership in 2017, Mr Cameron struck a domestic political blow, bringing greater unity to his party, depriving the UK Independence Party of their existential grievance, and throwing Labour's European policy into obstructive incoherence. (The Times 2013e)
> **May:** the Conservative party has embarked on one of its periodic bouts of soul-searching and division over Europe. Splits on Europe deprived the Tories of the political benefits of an improving economy in the 1990s. They could do so again. Worse for the prime minister, the danger for him is that

he is cast in the John Major role, frozen into indecision by the impossibility of reconciling the pro and anti European wings of his party. (The Times 2013d)

Regarding the "UKIP effect," John Denham (L) argues that "There is no doubt that this whole exercise is driven by the Conservative party's terror of UKIP" (Hansard 2013–2014a:565 col. 1197). Whilst Ian Davidson (L) notes that "it is really UKIP that has to be congratulated on this Bill. This would not be coming forward in this way if the Conservatives were not under pressure from UKIP" (ibid:1204). The *Daily Mirror* also argues that "Conservative Cabinet Ministers queuing up to claim they'd vote to leave Europe if a referendum was held now is a victory for Nigel Farage" (Daily Mirror 2013b). Although the focus is, to a major extent, on the Conservatives, James Wharton (C) states that "The truth is that the Labour party is split down the middle on this issue, because it knows that the British people want and deserve a say, but its leader is too weak to lead and refuses to offer it direction" (Hansard 2013–2014a:565 col. 1177).

Although the focus of attention has moved from Labour in 1975 to the Conservatives in 1992–1993 and 2013, it is an element of continuity that it is the party of government that comes under scrutiny in each occasion. Once again the European issue presents a political threat to party unity and prime-ministerial authority.

5.7   Chapter Conclusion

Pro-European voices occupy a minor part of the discourse of 2013. It is Eurosceptics of both, the more qualified, "soft" variety like the Prime Minister and the outright rejectionist, "hard" Eurosceptics like Nigel Farage who predominate. Of the three major themes, Economy, Jobs, and Prosperity has lesser importance in the discourse than Immigration or Sovereignty and Democracy. The latter two are linked, with immigration from the EU presented as a threat to the sovereignty of the UK by Farage and a number of media editorials.

The discourse of 2013 displays some elements of continuity from 1992 to 1993 and 1975. Sovereignty and Democracy persists as a major theme, with Eurosceptics continuing to argue in terms of the anti-democratic nature of the EU and the threat it poses to national sovereignty. Economic issues are also to the fore, with arguments once again featuring uncertainty and concerns about balance of trade. An important change in the discourse is that immigration has become a major part of the debate since 1992–1993, when it appeared as a minor theme. The stereotyping of people from Romania and Bulgaria as criminals and illegitimate welfare recipients is, if not dominant in the discourse, in a strong enough position to be particularly striking. The implications of both these continuities and the growth in importance of immigration as an issue in the discourse will be addressed in the concluding chapter.

NOTES

1. A House of Commons Background Paper explains Private Members' Bills as follows: "Private Members' Bills are presented by individual MPs or members of the House of Lords ('private Members'). They must go through the same procedures as Government bills in order to become law, but much less time is made available for them in the Parliamentary calendar. Most of them fail because there is not enough time for them to progress, rather than because of active opposition" (House of Commons 2012:14).
2. Once again assembled in a Word document to enable straightforward reading and searching.

REFERENCES

Alexandre-Collier, A. (2015). Reassessing British conservative Euroscepticism as a case of party (mis)management. In K. Tournier-Sol & C. Gifford (Eds.), *The UK challenge to Europeanization: The persistence of British Euroscepticism*. Basingstoke: Palgrave Macmillan.

Balzacq, T. (2012). The Routledge handbook of security studies. In M. Dunn Cavelty & V. Mauer (Eds.), *Routledge handbooks* (pp. xvi, 482 p.). London: Routledge.

Buonfino, A. (2004). Between unity and plurality: The politicization and securitization of the discourse of immigration in Europe. *New Political Science, 26*(1), 23–49.

Cameron, D. (2012, June 30). David Cameron: We need to be clear about the best way of getting what is best for Britain. *The Daily Telegraph.*

Cameron, D. (2013). David Cameron's speech on the EU: Full text. *The New Statesman.* Retrieved January 10, 2013, from http://www.newstatesman.com/politics/2013/01/david-camerons-speech-eu-full-text

Cowley, P., & Stuart, M. (2012). The cambusters: The conservative European Union referendum rebellion of October 2011. *The Political Quarterly, 83*(2), 402–406.

Daddow, O. (2006). Euroscepticism and the culture of the discipline of history. *Review of International Studies, 32*(2), 309–328.

Daddow, O. (2015a). Interpreting the outsider tradition in British European policy speeches from Thatcher to Cameron. *JCMS: Journal of Common Market Studies, 53*(1), 71–88.

Daddow, O. (2015b). Performing Euroscepticism: The UK press and Cameron's Bloomberg speech. In K. Tournier-Sol & C. Gifford (Eds.), *The UK challenge to Europeanization: The Persistence of British Euroscepticism*. Basingstoke: Palgrave Macmillan.

Daily Mail. (2013a, November 22). Brussels and why Mr Cameron can no longer ignore the people on immigration. *Daily Mail.*

Daily Mail. (2013b, September 13). EU must be joking! *Daily Mail.*

Daily Mail. (2013c, November 7). We don't have room for another London. *Daily Mail.*

Daily Mirror. (2013a, January 24). Cam's EU gamble. *Daily Mirror.*

Daily Mirror. (2013b, May 13). EU-less lot. *Daily Mirror.*

Daily Mirror. (2013c, May 17). EU fixation. *Daily Mirror.*

Daily Mirror. (2013d, November 28). EU nasty man, Cam. *Daily Mirror.*

Daily Mirror. (2013e, January 23). Voters are EU ready? *Daily Mirror.*

de Wilde, P., Michailidou, A., & Trenz, H.-J. (2014). Converging on Euroscepticism: Online polity contestation during European parliament elections. *European Journal of Political Research, 53*(4), 766–783.

Farage, N. (2013). Nigel Farage's speech at the UKIP conference—full text and audio. *The Spectator.* Retrieved April 7, from http://blogs.spectator.co.uk/coffeehouse/2013/09/nigel-farages-speech-full-text-and-audio/

Forman, F. N. (2003). *Constitutional change in the United Kingdom*. London: Routledge. xviii, 414 pages pp.

Hansard. (2013–2014a). *House of Commons Debates* (Vol. 565), Col. 1169–1251.

Hansard. (2013–2014b). *House of Commons Debates* (Vol. 571), Col. 528–584.

Hawkins, B. (2012). Nation, separation and threat: An analysis of British media discourses on the European Union treaty reform process. *JCMS: Journal of Common Market Studies, 50*(4), 561–577.

House of Commons. (2012). *House of Commons background paper: Public bills in parliament*. London: Parliament & Constitution Centre, House of Commons Library.

Huysmans, J. (2000). The European Union and the securitization of migration. *JCMS: Journal of Common Market Studies, 38*(5), 751–777.

Lynch, P. (2015). Conservative modernisation and European integration: From silence to salience and schism. *British Politics, 10*(2), 185–203.

Macmillan, C. (2015). British political discourse on the EU in the context of the Eurozone crisis. In K. Tournier-Sol & C. Gifford (Eds.), *The UK challenge to*

Europeanization: The persistence of British Euroscepticism. Basingstoke: Palgrave Macmillan.

Marcussen, M., Risse, T., Engelmann-Martin, D., Knopf, H. J., & Roscher, K. (1999). Constructing Europe? The evolution of French, British and German nation state identities. *Journal of European Public Policy, 6*(4), 614–633.

Montgomerie, T. (2012). 100 Tory MPs call for Cameron to prepare legislation for EU referendum. ConservativeHome.Retrieved May 12, from http://www.conservativehome.com/thetorydiary/2012/06/100-tory-mps-call-for-cameron-to-prepare-legislation-for-eu-referendum.html

Neumann, I. B. (1999). *Uses of the other: "The East" in European identity formation.* Manchester: Manchester University Press. xv, 281 p. pp.

Seldon, A., & Snowdon, P. (2015). *Cameron at 10: The inside story 2010–2015* (Kindle ed.). London: HarperCollins Publishers.

Spiering, M. (2002). Eurosceptic concerns about national identity in the European Union. *International Area Studies Review, 5*(1), 69–80.

The Sun. (2013a, January 17). Border alert. *The Sun.*

The Sun. (2013b, January 24). Game changer. *The Sun.*

The Sun. (2013c, January 25). It's EUr shout. *The Sun.*

The Sun. (2013d, January 6). Psst, Dave …hurry up! *The Sun.*

The Times. (2013a, March 5). Boundaries of welfare. *The Times.*

The Times. (2013b, March 3). Europe hits the self-destruct button. *The Times.*

The Times. (2013c, June 2). Europe picks a fight and leads with its jaw. *The Times.*

The Times. (2013d, May 12). Even Europeans should be sceptics now. *The Times.*

The Times. (2013e, January 24). In or out. *The Times.*

Tournier-Sol, K. (2015a). The UKIP Challenge. In Tournier-Sol, K. & Gifford, C. (eds) *The UK Challenge to Europeanization: The Persistence of British Euroscepticism.* Basingstoke: Palgrave Macmillan.

Tournier-Sol, K. (2015b). Reworking the Eurosceptic and Conservative Traditions into a Populist Narrative: UKIP's Winning Formula? *JCMS: Journal of Common Market Studies, 53*(1): 140–156.

Vail, M. I. (2015). Between one-nation Toryism and neoliberalism: The dilemmas of British conservatism and Britain's evolving place in Europe. *JCMS: Journal of Common Market Studies, 53*(1), 106–122.

Wintour, P., & Watt, N. (2013, 16 May). EU referendum: Cameron snubbed by 114 Tory MPs over Queens' speech. *The Guardian.*

CHAPTER 6

Conclusion: Struggling over Sovereignty

Abstract The chapter sums up 40 years of the UK's discursive struggle over Europe, overviewing both key continuities and the key changes since the 1975 referendum. Historical allusions of invasion, worries about loss of sovereignty, and implicit and explicit threats to national identity feature throughout the three periods, whilst the position of Euroscepticism within the media discourse has strengthened considerably. The chapter describes how these factors, in combination with the growth in pertinence of immigration issues, will have implications for the referendum campaign, which will likely come down to whether the fears of the economic impact of a Brexit trump the fears of immigration and sovereignty under threat.

Keywords The Continental other • Sovereignty • Project Fear

This book studies the evolution of the British discourse on Europe since the 1970s. Taken together, the three periods studied here, 1975, 1992–1993, and 2013 (Chaps. 3, 4, and 5), provide material that adds important value to understanding how Prime Minister David Cameron's referendum commitment "became logically possible" (Bartelson 1995:8). In theoretical terms, this book demonstrates that a poststructuralist approach to discourse analysis provides useful insight into the mutually constitutive nature of foreign policy and identity.

J. Todd, *The UK's Relationship with Europe*,
DOI 10.1007/978-3-319-33669-5_6

107

I shall use this concluding chapter to draw out some discursive effects and potential implications for the UK's relationship with Europe, with a focus on the forthcoming in/out referendum. This will be achieved by analysing both the overall nature of the evolving discourse and the rising importance of immigration, which has gone from being essentially absent in the British discourse on Europe in 1975 to being a major issue at present. I will present an overview of both the key *continuities* and the key *changes* in the discourse. Such an overview gives an impression for how the "battle for truth" over the framing of the British relationship with Europe evolved over the past 40 years. Before this, I shall show how the Continental other has been represented across the three periods under analysis. This provides a basis from which to draw out some key implications for the referendum campaign, founded upon the theoretical perspective that identity and foreign policy are mutually constitutive. The discourse analysed in this study included many explicit calls to action (often a "Brexit" from the EU) on the basis of a particular construction of British identity. With this perspective in mind, it is possible to propose some implications for how the UK will come to relate to Europe on the basis of the representations of identity in the discourse.

6.1   The Continental Other

This subsection sums up how the Continental other has been constructed over the period under analysis. Figure 6.1 shows the key aspects of this other as constructed by those opposed to EEC/EU membership across the three peaks in the discourse. Loosely based on Hansen's graphic representation method (see Sect. 2.5.2), it shows how the Continental other is linked to a range of negative attributes in order to differentiate it from the British self. There are a number of important continuities. Primarily, Europe is consistently represented as anti-democratic, with Eurosceptics attaching a range of related attributes like authoritarian and secretive (1975), unelected and unaccountable (1992–1993), and power-hungry and a threat to national identity (2013) to their version of the Continental other. Also attributed to this other are, to a somewhat lesser extent, inflexibility/rigidity and bureaucracy. In 2013, a new attribute of being a source of immigration is attached to the Continental other. These issues will be addressed in more detail below.

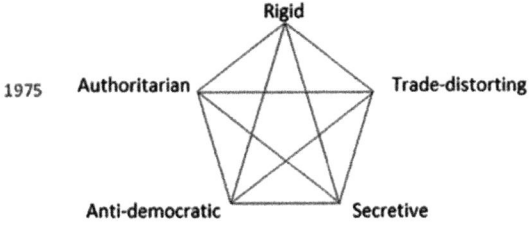

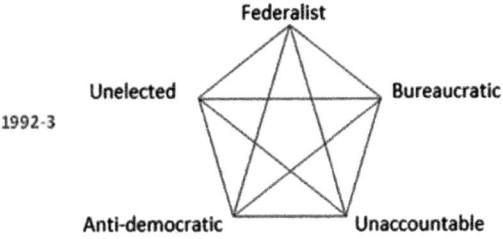

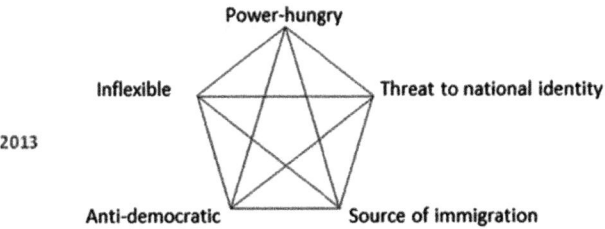

Fig. 6.1   British representations of the Continental other

6.2   KEY CONTINUITIES AND KEY CHANGES

This section summarises the most important changes and continuities in the British discourse on Europe as described in my first research question. There are three important *continuities* to highlight: first, the persistence of Sovereignty and Democracy as a major theme in the discourse; second, the similar constancy of presence of economic issues; and third, the continuity of the discourse's tone, which is run through with references to threat and danger. The persistence of debates on issues of sovereignty and democracy are, at one level, understandable given the nature of EEC/EU membership. The UK is not the only country to have Eurosceptic voices raising concerns about issues of sovereignty and democratic deficit.[1] But when the political and media discourse consistently includes strong-to-dominant voices that frame the EU as an anti-democratic, unelected Continental other, this affects both people's opinions about Europe and politicians' bandwidth of possible choices, to paraphrase Neumann (2008:62). This shows how the discourse "worked" so that David Cameron was gradually forced into making the referendum commitment.

The consistent salience of economic issues is also interesting, if not surprising, given their status as the starting point and main focus of the European integration process. One point it throws up reinforces the notion that discourse is produced within—and affects—a context. The context for all three of the peaks in the discourse here involved a recession. There ensued in each case a battle for truth regarding whether European membership was the root cause of the problem or a necessary part of the solution.

Finally, the continuity of tone is very important. The negative dominates the positive across all three periods of analysis, both on the pro-Europe side and, to an even greater extent, on the Eurosceptic side. Historical allusions of invasion, worries about loss of sovereignty, and implicit and explicit threats to national identity and the self (both individual and collective) feature throughout the three periods. Again, these concerns feature in other countries too (see, in particular, Spiering 2002). Huysmans and Buonfino (2008:766), when analysing the British discourse on migration and security, speak of "a politics of unease," which, I would argue, permeates the broader discourse on Europe as well.

There are three key *changes* over the period of analysis to highlight. The first is that immigration has gone from being almost entirely absent from the discourse in 1975, to a minor issue in 1992–1993, to a major theme in 2013. The second change is a shift from the Labour Party being the most divided political party on the European issue in 1975 to the Conservatives being the most divided in 1992–1993 and 2013. That being said, the implications of Jeremy Corbyn's election as leader of the Labour Party and the accompanying reinvigoration of the hard left are as yet unclear when it comes to the forthcoming referendum campaign. The third change is that the newspapers' editorial stance has become markedly more Eurosceptic over the 40 years under analysis.

With regard to the growth in pertinence of immigration, there are two plausible analyses. The first is that each of the three periods analysed has an "issue of the day" that is informed by the context of the period and forms a major theme in the discourse. In 1975, this was Agriculture, Food, and Fisheries, in 1992–1993 it was Centralisation, Federalisation, and Subsidiarity, and in 2013 it was Immigration. Under this analysis, a new issue may well crop up in the future and take over immigration's prominent place in the discourse. However, my view is that a second scenario is more likely. The immigration debates have deep roots in the negative tone of the discourse mentioned earlier. Forty years of threats to national identity, fears of British democracy at risk, and so on, have provided fertile ground in which EU-linked anti-immigration rhetoric has taken root. A number of scholars have spoken of the securitisation of migration in Europe (see Buonfino 2004; Huysmans 2006), and such securitising moves are more easily accomplished in a discursive context where threats and fears have been present for many years. This is a less optimistic take on the issue, but it is reasonable to assert that immigration will continue to form a major element of the European discourse for the foreseeable future, not least given the additional factor of the ongoing refugee crisis.

The second change—the location of party divisions—requires less analysis, in that whilst the Labour Party continues to have a number of Eurosceptic MPs, it is now much less divided than the Conservatives. This can in part be explained by Labour's move towards the centre ground during the 1980s and 1990s[2] (see Daniels 1998), whilst many Conservatives followed Margaret Thatcher in her journey from pro-European to becoming the mother of Euroscepticism (see Lynch and Whitaker 2013). The Conservative Party divisions have obviously had an effect in helping push David Cameron into his referendum commitment and will, as detailed in the following section, have an effect on the referendum campaign.

The third change, with newspapers like *The Times* moving from a pro-Europe to Eurosceptic editorial stance, means that Euroscepticism are markedly more dominant in the discourse than before. Crowley describes this current situation as "Eurosceptic discursive hegemony" (2015:location 1643). This is, in part, down to the Eurosceptic views of newspaper owners like Rupert Murdoch (see Anderson 2004), though I would argue that there are also more complex processes of mutual constitution between popular opinion and the discourse of politicians and the media at work here. Daddow (2012) has described this as a move in the media from "permissive consensus" to "destructive dissent" concerning European integration over this period: the over 220 editorials analysed as part of this study would align with Daddow's description. The strengthened position of Euroscepticism within the media discourse will also have implications for the referendum campaign.

6.3   EFFECTS AND IMPLICATIONS

This final section will set out some effects and suggest a number of implications for the future on the basis of the preceding analysis. The first, rather obvious, effect of the consistent differentiation between a democratic British self and anti-democratic Continental other (not to mention the continuity of negative tone) in the discourse is the referendum itself. It is noteworthy that, despite other European countries showing high levels of Euroscepticism (see Torreblanca and Leonard 2013), only the UK engaged in renegotiating its relationship with the EU and only the British Prime Minister committed to holding a referendum on membership. The genealogical approach I took shows how this sense of British difference and exceptionalism, crystallised by the referendum commitment, has developed over the past 40 years. Wallace (2013:546) similarly notes that "[t]he tendency towards British exceptionalism has become more pronounced across the years." The differentiation between self and other employed all three of Hansen's (2006) dimensions of identity: spatial, temporal, and ethical, employing both explicit and implicit intertextuality. Eurosceptics, both "soft" like David Cameron, and "hard" like Nigel Farage, use differentiation to discursively position the self/other slash at the English Channel (see Fig. 6.2).

The increasing prominence of immigration in the discourse—and the rise of UKIP—also have important implications. These two phenomena exist in a rather unfortunate and mutually productive (or indeed destructive) relationship. UKIP has been able to effectively link immigration with EU membership, deploying right-wing populist rhetoric to build their profile and electoral support. Conservative ministers have, in an attempt to cut off UKIP's rise, employed anti-immigration rhetoric and proposed anti-immigration policies (see Partos and Bale 2015). Such policies and rhetoric serve to legitimise anti-immigration opinion.

Looking ahead to the referendum campaign, it is worth observing from the Scottish independence debates that referendum campaigns can

Fig. 6.2   British self/Continental other

be highly unpredictable. Most commentators (and opinion polls) fore-
casted a fairly safe majority against Scottish independence at the start of
the campaign. However, the polls narrowed markedly towards the end of
the campaign (see, e.g. Curtice 2014), and the eventual vote in favour of
maintaining the Union was in doubt right up to polling day itself.[3] With
regard to a referendum on EU membership, the gambit of renegotiation
followed by a referendum, which by-and-large worked for Harold Wilson in
1975, will be more difficult to achieve for David Cameron. The consistent
divide between a British self and Continental other over the intervening
period has been strongly reinforced by the anti-immigration representation and its employment of welfare chauvinism. As Daddow (2015:85)
notes, "withdrawal from the EU would be more in line with expressed
British identity constructions than would continued EU membership."

   The implications of the presence of so many hard Eurosceptics within
the Conservative Party must also be considered. Not only will such

Eurosceptics continue the self/other differentiation, but with their party alone in government (i.e. without the pro-European Liberal Democrats), they will do so in a manner that continues to narrow the Prime Minister's bandwidth of options. This could mean less room to manoeuvre in the renegotiations and/or how their results are presented. David Cameron's early announcement that he plans to suspend the Cabinet's collective responsibility is an indicator of the internecine difficulties ahead.

It will be fascinating to observe how the discursive struggle of the referendum campaign plays out. How will the Prime Minister seek to make the best of his renegotiation? Will the fears of the economic impact of a Brexit trump the fears of immigration and sovereignty under threat? It seems likely that this is ultimately what the referendum campaign will boil down to. Whilst a battle between two "Project Fears" seems a rather unedifying manner to decide an issue of such importance, insecure exceptionalism does seem like it will predominate on both sides of the debate.

NOTES

1. For an analysis of Euroscepticism in Central and Eastern Europe, see Taggart and Szczerbiak (2001), for Scandinavia see Sitter (2001), and for a general overview (including Germany) see Spiering (2002).
2. Of course, since Jeremy Corbyn's assumption of the role of Labour Party leader, the party's drift to the centre has been arrested and is beginning to reverse.
3. It is worth observing that a vote in favour of leaving the EU would, in all likelihood, precipitate more than one painful break-up: the UK leaving the EU followed by Scotland leaving the UK.

REFERENCES

Anderson, P. J. (2004). A flag of convenience? Discourse and motivations of the London-based Eurosceptic Press. *European Studies: A Journal of European Culture, History and Politics, 20*(1), 151–170.

Bartelson, J. (1995). *A genealogy of sovereignty*. Cambridge studies in international relations. Cambridge: Cambridge University Press. x, 317 p. pp.

Buonfino, A. (2004). Between unity and plurality: The politicization and securitization of the discourse of immigration in Europe. *New Political Science, 26*(1), 23–49.

Crowley, C. (2015). British Euroscepticism and the geopolitics of a post-imperial Britain. In K. Tournier-Sol & C. Gifford (Eds.), *The UK challenge to*

Europeanization: The persistence of British Euroscepticism. Basingstoke: Palgrave Macmillan.

Curtice, J. (2014). *Easter polls offer further hope for yes.* What Scotland thinks. Retrieved April 23, 2014, from http://blog.whatscotlandthinks. org/2014/04/easter-polls-offer-further-hope-for-yes/

Daddow, O. (2012). The UK media and 'Europe': From permissive consensus to destructive dissent. *International Affairs, 88*(6), 1219–1236.

Daddow, O. (2015). Interpreting the outsider tradition in British European policy speeches from Thatcher to Cameron. *JCMS: Journal of Common Market Studies, 53*(1), 71–88.

Daniels, P. (1998). From hostility to 'constructive engagement': The Europeanisation of the labour party. *West European Politics, 21*(1), 72–96.

Hansen, L. (2006). *Security as practice: Discourse analysis and the Bosnian war.* London: Routledge. xxiii, 259 p. pp.

Huysmans, J. (2006). *The politics of insecurity: Fear, migration, and asylum in the EU.* The new international relations. Oxon: Routledge.

Huysmans, J., & Buonfino, A. (2008). Politics of exception and unease: Immigration, asylum and terrorism in parliamentary debates in the UK. *Political Studies, 56*(4), 766–788.

Lynch, P., & Whitaker, R. (2013). Where there is discord, can they bring harmony? Managing intra-party dissent on European integration in the Conservative Party. *The British Journal of Politics & International Relations, 15*(3), 317–339.

Neumann, I. B. (2008). Discourse analysis. In A. Klotz & D. Prakash (Eds.), *Qualitative methods in international relations: A pluralist guide* (pp. xii, 260 p.). Basingstoke: Palgrave Macmillan.

Partos, R., & Bale, T. (2015). Immigration and asylum policy under Cameron's Conservatives. *British Politics, 10*(2), 169–184.

Sitter, N. (2001). The politics of opposition and European integration in Scandinavia: Is Euro-scepticism a government-opposition dynamic? *West European Politics, 24*(4), 22–39.

Spiering, M. (2002). Eurosceptic concerns about national identity in the European Union. *International Area Studies Review, 5*(1), 69–80.

Taggart, P. A., & Szczerbiak, A. (2001). *Parties, positions and Europe: Euroscepticism in the EU candidate states of Central and Eastern Europe.* Brighton: Sussex European Institute. 38 p. pp.

Torreblanca, J. I., & Leonard, M. (2013). The continent-wide rise of Euroscepticism. *The European Council on Foreign Relations.* London. 79.

Wallace, H. (2013). The UK: 40 Years of EU membership. *Journal of Contemporary European Research, 8*(4), pp. 531–546.

References

Alexandre-Collier, A. (2015). Reassessing British conservative Euroscepticism as a case of party (mis)management. In K. Tournier-Sol & C. Gifford (Eds.), *The UK challenge to Europeanization: The persistence of British Euroscepticism.* Palgrave Macmillan: Basingstoke.

Balzacq, T. (2012). The Routledge handbook of security studies. In M. Dunn Cavelty & V. Mauer (Eds.), *Routledge handbooks.* London: Routledge. pp. xvi, 482 p.

Cowley, P., & Stuart, M. (2012). The cambusters: The conservative European Union referendum rebellion of October 2011. *The Political Quarterly, 83*(2), 402–406.

Daddow, O. (2015b). Performing Euroscepticism: The UK press and Cameron's Bloomberg speech. In K. Tournier-Sol & C. Gifford (Eds.), *The UK challenge to Europeanization: The Persistence of British Euroscepticism.* Basingstoke: Palgrave Macmillan.

Daily Mail. (2013a, November 22). Brussels and why Mr Cameron can no longer ignore the people on immigration. *Daily Mail.*

Daily Mail. (2013b, September 13). EU must be joking! *Daily Mail.*

Daily Mail. (2013c, November 7). We don't have room for another London. *Daily Mail.*

Daily Mirror. (2013a, January 24). Cam's EU gamble. *Daily Mirror.*

Daily Mirror. (2013b, May 13). EU-less lot. *Daily Mirror.*

Daily Mirror. (2013c, May 17). EU fixation. *Daily Mirror.*

Daily Mirror. (2013d, November 28). EU nasty man, Cam. *Daily Mirror.*

Daily Mirror. (2013e, January 23). Voters are EU ready? *Daily Mirror.*

© The Editor(s) (if applicable) and The Author(s) 2016   117
J. Todd, *The UK's Relationship with Europe,*
DOI 10.1007/978-3-319-33669-5

de Wilde, P., Michailidou, A., & Trenz, H.-J. (2014). Converging on Euroscepticism: Online polity contestation during European parliament elections. *European Journal of Political Research, 53*(4), 766–783.

Diez, T. (1997). Review of the book *Foreign Policy and Discourse Analysis: France, Britain and Europe. Millennium-Journal of International Studies, 26*(3), 931–933.

Farage, N. (2013). Nigel Farage's speech at the UKIP conference—full text and audio. *The Spectator.* http://blogs.spectator.co.uk/coffeehouse/2013/09/nigel-farages-speech-full-text-and-audio/. Accessed 7 April.

Forman, F. N. (2003). *Constitutional change in the United Kingdom.* London: Routledge. xviii, 414 pages pp.

Hansard. (1992–1993a). *House of Commons Debates* (Vol. 208).

Hansard. (1992–1993b). *House of Commons Debates* (Vol. 229).

Hawkins, B. (2012). Nation, separation and threat: An analysis of British media discourses on the European Union treaty reform process. *JCMS: Journal of Common Market Studies, 50*(4), 561–577.

House of Commons. (2012). *House of Commons background paper: Public bills in parliament.* London: Parliament & Constitution Centre, House of Commons Library.

Lynch, P. (2015). Conservative modernisation and European integration: From silence to salience and schism. *British Politics, 10*(2), 185–203.

Macmillan, C. (2015). British political discourse on the EU in the context of the Eurozone crisis. In K. Tournier-Sol & C. Gifford (Eds.), *The UK challenge to Europeanization: The persistence of British Euroscepticism.* Basingstoke: Palgrave Macmillan.

The Sun. (2013a, January 17). Border alert. *The Sun.*

The Sun. (2013b, January 24). Game changer. *The Sun.*

The Sun. (2013c, January 25). It's EUr shout. *The Sun.*

The Sun. (2013d, January 6). Psst, Dave …hurry up! *The Sun.*

The Times. (2013a, March 5). Boundaries of welfare. *The Times.*

The Times. (2013b, March 3). Europe hits the self-destruct button. *The Times.*

The Times. (2013c, June 2). Europe picks a fight and leads with its jaw. *The Times.*

The Times. (2013d, May 12). Even Europeans should be sceptics now. *The Times.*

The Times. (2013e, January 24). In or out. *The Times.*

Torreblanca, J. I. L., & Mark. L. (2013). The European Council on Foreign Relations. The remarkable rise of continental Euroscepticism. http://ecfr.eu/content/entry/commentary_the_remarkable_rise_of_continental_euroscepticism129. Accessed 29 April.

Tournier-Sol, K. (2015a). Reworking the Eurosceptic and conservative traditions into a populist narrative: UKIP's winning formula? *JCMS: Journal of Common Market Studies, 53*(1), 140–156.

Tournier-Sol, K. (2015b). The UKIP Challenge. In K. Tournier-Sol & C. Gifford (Eds.), *The UK challenge to Europeanization: The persistence of British Euroscepticism*. Basingstoke: Palgrave Macmillan.

Vail, M. I. (2015). Between one-nation Toryism and neoliberalism: The dilemmas of British conservatism and Britain's evolving place in Europe. *JCMS: Journal of Common Market Studies, 53*(1), 106–122.

Wintour, P., & Watt, N. (2013, 16 May). EU referendum: Cameron snubbed by 114 Tory MPs over Queens' speech. *The Guardian*.

INDEX

Printed by Printforce, the Netherlands